DESIGNING & REMODELING
KITCHENS

Created and designed by
the editorial staff of
ORTHO BOOKS

Project Editor
Jill Fox

Writer
Robert J. Beckstrom

Photographer
Kenneth Rice

Illustrator
Rik Olson

Ortho Books

Publisher
Edward A. Evans

Editorial Director
Christine Jordan

Production Director
Ernie S. Tasaki

Managing Editors
Michael D. Smith
Sally W. Smith

System Manager
Linda M. Bouchard

National Sales Manager
J. D. Gillis

National Accounts Manager—
Book Trade
Paul D. Wiedemann

Marketing Specialist
Dennis M. Castle

Distribution Specialist
Barbara F. Steadham

Operations Assistant
Georgiann Wright

Administrative Assistant
Francine Lorentz-Olson

Senior Technical Analyst
J. A. Crozier, Jr., Ph.D.

Address all inquiries to
Ortho Books
Box 5006
San Ramon CA 94583-0906

Copyright © 1982, 1990
Monsanto Company
All rights reserved under international and
Pan-American copyright conventions.

11	12	13

98

ISBN 0-89721-216-9
Library of Congress Catalog Card
Number 89-85931

THE SOLARIS GROUP
2527 Camino Ramon
San Ramon, CA 94583-0906

Acknowledgments

Special Design Consultant
Beverly Wilson, CKD

Kitchen Consultants
Fred Brasch, Superior Remodeling
Lyndell Hogan and Paul Klein, House
 of Kitchens
Kathleen Donohue and Lois Shamberger,
 Neil Kelly Construction
David Newton, CKD, National Kitchen
 and Bath Association
Don Riley, Heritage Woodworks
Lee Seronello, Kitchen and Bath Designs

Special Thanks to
Linda Beckstrom

Photography Assistants
Norma Bontadelli
Melissa McCumiskey

Copy Chief
Melinda E. Levine

Editorial Coordinator
Cass Dempsey

Copyeditor
Irene Elmer

Proofreader
Karen K. Johnson

Indexer
Elinor Lindheimer

Editorial Assistants
Nicole Barrett
Deborah Bruner
Marci Smith

Composition by
Tamara Mallory

Systems Coordinator
Laurie A. Steele

Production by
Lezlly Freier

Separations by
Creative Color

Lithographed in the USA by
Banta Company

Front cover: Hand-painted tiles—like those covering the vent/hood in this kitchen—have decorated homes since the days of Alexander the Great.

Page 1: The desire to display their prized collection of World War I–era Victory Garden posters prompted these homeowners to eliminate wall cabinets from their kitchen design. Storage needs are handled by large pantry-style cupboards on the opposite wall.

Page 3: Consider the adjoining room when determining your kitchen design. Matching wallpaper in the kitchen and breakfast room pulls together the related rooms into a complete dining suite.

Back cover
Top left: Planning ways to save steps when cooking is an important aspect of kitchen design. Open shelves next to this oven contain often-used baking sheets.

Top right: Color is an important element of kitchen design. This kitchen is monochromatic, but it is enlivened with colorful accessories.

Bottom left: This remodeling project involved tearing out walls to turn a web of small, dark rooms into a bright, expansive kitchen.

Bottom right: Adding a second sink and countertop in a formerly unused corner provided these homeowners with an extra food preparation area and a handy bar for entertaining.

DESIGNING & REMODELING
KITCHENS

PREFACE

The kitchen is the center of most homes—the hub of daily activity, the focus of family living, a place where important events are celebrated and precious memories begin.

If you are like most homeowners, you probably spend more time in the kitchen than anywhere else in your house. Family members wander in and out; friends sit there to visit; and party guests always seem to migrate to the kitchen, even when you've made elaborate arrangements to lure them elsewhere. If you're a serious food lover, your kitchen is especially important to you. For these reasons you probably want that kitchen to be as attractive, efficient, and pleasant as possible, and you may be thinking about remodeling it.

You are in good company. Kitchen remodeling is the most popular type of home improvement in the United States, and it is becoming even more popular as more and more people elect to upgrade their present home rather than buy a new one. Very often the first project they consider is a new kitchen. Creating that kitchen is what this book is all about.

Maybe you are trying to do today's work in yesterday's kitchen. Are you running yourself ragged in a huge space meant for a large family, or are you cramped in a small postwar tract-house kitchen with outdated appliances and inconvenient fixtures? Maybe your kitchen works fairly well, but it needs improved lighting or energy-saving appliances. Whatever your situation, you have probably already said to yourself, "Something must be done." The next step is to decide how much you can do, how much it will cost, what skills you will need, and where you can go for help.

Your budget may rule out a total renovation. Remodeling means different things to different people. It can mean adding a few shelves and applying a fresh coat of paint, or it can mean a substantial overhaul, requiring skills in carpentry, plumbing, and wiring. The guidelines presented here can be used for any project. Although remodeling a kitchen is not a job to undertake lightly, you will find that everything falls into place if you take your time and break the work down into steps.

If you lack basic construction skills and have never done any home remodeling before, consider taking on some smaller projects first, or get help from friends, neighbors, or professional tradespeople before undertaking as large a project as a complete kitchen remodeling.

This book will guide you through a complete kitchen remodeling. The first chapter presents ideas and techniques for planning and designing a new kitchen, using your present kitchen as a point of departure.

The second chapter is a portfolio of recently remodeled kitchens—real kitchens that have been transformed from drab, ordinary rooms into successful work spaces with loads of personalized appeal. Reading about these projects, studying the floor plans, and looking at the photographs will inspire you to set your own goals—and to reach them.

The third chapter presents techniques for managing a kitchen remodeling project. Whether you hire professionals or do the work yourself, you will find useful information here on purchasing materials, estimating costs, obtaining permits, working with professionals, and scheduling the project.

The last chapter is a comprehensive construction guide with step-by-step instructions for removing old fixtures and appliances and installing new ones. This chapter focuses on tasks that are unique to kitchen remodeling, but it includes summary information on more general skills, such as carpentry, rough plumbing, rough wiring, painting, laying tile, and installing flooring.

This book will help you to enjoy the process of creating an efficient, attractive kitchen. Read through the entire book before you start your project. The planning will be easier if you understand the details of installation, and knowing the basics about design will help you when it's time to do the construction.

__Opposite:__ The sleek, hard texture of a granite countertop is tempered by the wood of the butcher-block center island in this contemporary kitchen. A well-defined combination of textures is one mark of a balanced design.

KITCHEN DESIGN

Beautiful and well-designed kitchens are not created merely by shopping for good-looking fixtures and installing them. The key to a successful kitchen remodeling is careful planning. Allow weeks, even months, for this process. You'll want time to absorb new ideas and to analyze preliminary designs. There will be big decisions to make and small details to consider. This chapter begins with an overview of the design process and then presents sources for gathering ideas. Designing your new kitchen starts with making a survey of your present kitchen and an inventory of your life-style as it pertains to your kitchen use. Also included in this chapter are basic design principles and a rundown of popular kitchen styles. Even if you work with a professional designer, you'll benefit from following these guidelines. If you plan to do the entire design yourself, you'll want to check the section on designing the new kitchen, which provides a step-by-step plan for layout and plan drawing. Review, as well, the section on specifying materials and equipment, which will help you choose finishes and fixtures to create the kitchen of your dreams.

Rich wood cabinets, handmade tile, and displays of crafted items create an American country theme in this traditional-style kitchen. The spice rack built into the back splash near the cooktop makes excellent use of an often underutilized space.

DESIGN OVERVIEW

Designing a kitchen is a complex but not mysterious process. It involves a systematic and thorough analysis of the problems and a patient search for the best solutions.

It is easy to put all your emphasis on the product—the final design—but let yourself enjoy the process as you do it.

Designing a new kitchen is like designing anything else. The basic rules are the same. Find out as much as you can. Be willing to make decisions. Don't be afraid to get help.

The following checklist is a summary of this chapter. It takes you through a typical design process, step by step. In practice, however, the design process is seldom linear. It is more like a spiral—that is, it takes you around in circles, but it brings you back to each step at a higher level of information and insight. You are constantly backtracking and repeating—and constantly learning.

Steps to Kitchen Design

Even if you are working with a professional designer, you can do the first three or four of the following steps yourself.

1. Draw the base plan of the existing kitchen to scale.
2. Gather information.
3. Survey the existing kitchen.
4. Inventory your life-style as it relates to the kitchen.
5. Set design goals.
6. Choose a kitchen style.
7. Draw several preliminary plans.
8. Determine your budget.
9. Specify materials and equipment.
10. Complete the new floor plan.
11. Make elevation drawings.
12. Refine the plan and specify details.

At some point you may feel overwhelmed by all these new facts and possibilities. Allow plenty of time for each stage. If necessary let the project rest while you assimilate the information that you will need in order to make the right decisions.

As examples of how others have handled various design challenges, the second chapter, which begins on page 38, profiles six kitchen remodeling projects and presents the finished kitchens. Seeing how others did it should help you through your own design process.

You may need to make additional adjustments after you've shopped for materials, obtained permits, and planned the construction. A project-planning overview designed to help you do this makes up the third chapter, which begins on page 62.

Above: *The steps involved in a successful kitchen design include major decisions, such as choosing an overall style and theme; choosing wallcoverings and tile accents; and deciding the little details, such as the placement of curios.*
Opposite: *When it is well planned, even a small kitchen can accommodate every major appliance and convenience desired in a modern home.*

GATHERING IDEAS

One of the first and most enjoyable tasks in designing is to gather ideas. You will quickly accumulate a pile of materials that you should organize to maintain a sense of order during planning. An accordion file (or two) works very well. Not only does it organize your notes, brochures, and clippings, but it will hold bulky items, such as magazines, tile samples, and color chips.

Other ways to organize your planning process include using file folders, scrapbooks, and three-ring binders. Use categories suggested by the page headings and checklists in this book, or devise your own system of classification.

If you find yourself overwhelmed by too much information, winnow it out. Discard ideas and products that you don't like. Clip photographs from brochures rather than filing the entire pamphlet. Be sure to save product specifications and installation instructions that you will need later on.

In designing a kitchen, there are many sources to which you can turn for inspiration.

Books and Magazines

If you have not already loaded up your supermarket cart with home-decorating magazines, do so now. Every one of them is full of innovative plans and new ways to use materials and products. You will find valuable information in both the advertisements and the feature articles of these magazines.

If you have access to a large public library or to the office of an architect or contractor, look over some of the magazines that are distributed only to the trade. Some manufacturers, such as hardware producers, advertise only in trade publications, and you will not get to see their products anywhere else.

Manufacturers' Brochures

Contact manufacturers to obtain information on their products. Their brochures, many of which are in color, include specification sheets that give actual dimensions and finishes, installation instructions, and lists of dealers in your general area.

See whether your local library carries *Sweet's Catalog*. This compilation of many brochures is put together for architects, designers, and builders. It contains hundreds of photographs and illustrations arranged by topic and manufacturer, and it can give you still more ideas about how to select and install kitchen products.

Professional Trade Associations

Manufacturing and professional associations often provide lists of local dealers. They may also produce informative booklets on how kitchen cabinets are made, how to install ceramic tile, or how to work with a kitchen designer. Most of them will not recommend individual manufacturers, suppliers, or professionals, but they can be of help in answering general questions.

Showrooms

One of the best ways to learn about specific products is to visit the showroom of a kitchen specialist, cabinet dealer, home improvement center, or other supplier offering kitchen fixtures. Although some outlets may sell only to contractors and other professionals, they often offer products that you might not find elsewhere. Catalogs and specifications are available, and you may be able to borrow sample chips or books so that you can consider the products more carefully at home. The showroom may also have a portfolio that you can browse through, featuring remodeled kitchens in your own community.

Kitchen Tours

Many organizations raise money by sponsoring home tours. Check the calendar section of your local newspaper for these events. Tours are an excellent way to get ideas; often the homeowner or the designer is available and is willing to answer questions. You will also notice how the kitchens "feel." This is a very important aspect of kitchen design and planning that is difficult to convey in photographs. Cooking classes held in a home-style kitchen will also enable you to experience good kitchen design at first hand.

Friends' Kitchens

Do not overlook your friends and family. When you visit their kitchens, observe how the space is arranged, what features you like, how activity centers are laid out, and how different lighting schemes work. You may find a gold mine of information just by asking, "What do you like about your kitchen?" If you plan to remodel parts of your own kitchen yourself, ask to look inside your friends' cabinets, under the sink, in the basement, behind the range, and elsewhere, to see how things are installed.

Reality Checks

Before you begin the actual design work, you should be aware of certain factors that will affect the project. It is easy to see these factors as limitations, as restrictions on your creativity, but they are really more like boundaries that define the arena of possibilities. They are the local building codes, your budget, and the structural integrity of the house. All are important and all must be addressed.

Checking Local Codes

In most municipalities a remodeling project is subject to certain codes. Depending on the type and scope of the work, these may include the zoning, building, plumbing, electrical, mechanical, and energy codes. Visit the planning or building inspection department and discuss your project

The cooktop countertop adds an interesting line to this narrow, galley-style kitchen. It also makes the burners at the back of the cooktop easier to reach. The narrow shelf above the countertop provides display space for often-used cooking ingredients.

with the appropriate officials to find out what codes pertain and what permits you will need. Some lending institutions require you to obtain all the permits before they will guarantee a home improvement loan. Occasionally, too, you could have trouble selling a home because remodeling projects were not done up to code.

Working to code is important. It ensures a safe job, and it gives you a sense of pride in a job well done.

Zoning and design restrictions generally apply to changes in the exterior of the house. Unless the project involves an addition or exterior alterations, it will probably not be subject to these restrictions.

A project will be subject to the building code if there are structural changes or if it exceeds a certain dollar amount. In either case you will probably have to get a permit. The building code covers structural and safety issues related to the actual construction. For a kitchen remodeling this is likely to include framing or structural alterations, minimum ceiling heights, clearance below beams, size of doorways, type of window glass, height of steps, clearances around cooktops, and safety equipment.

Plumbing, electrical, and mechanical codes cover all the work done in these respective areas, although replacing existing fixtures without moving the plumbing or wiring usually does not require a permit. Energy codes cover house and window insulation, weather stripping, and the use of energy-saving appliances and light fixtures.

It is not necessary to be versed in all the codes. Just be aware that they will govern some of the design and construction work. General codes are summarized in the fourth chapter. If you hire professionals to do the work, they will be responsible for obtaining permits, following the codes, and getting proper inspections.

Determining Your Budget

One of the first questions you will ask about the project is How much is it going to cost? The more realistic approach, as you begin to plan, is to determine how much you can spend. Investigate all your financing options early—equity home loans, home improvement loans, borrowing against certain assets. Find out how much money you qualify for, and under what terms. Consider any possible future income that might enable you to do the project in phases. In order to decrease stress later in your remodeling project, establish a firm and realistic figure for your budget as soon as possible.

Unfortunately, cost overruns are common in remodeling. Establish a budget that is at least 10 percent less than your reserves to allow for changes and unexpected complications. Remember that a beautiful and well-designed kitchen will enhance the resale value of your home. The money you spend on remodeling could turn out to be a good investment in a favorable real-estate market. You may want to just refinance your house to obtain the money for your remodeling project.

Making Structural Changes

Whether you are making minor structural changes—such as moving a sink, removing a water heater, or enlarging a window—or major changes, such as adding a room or relocating an interior wall, you must consider the structure of the house when you plan your design.

Do not rule out changes because you think they may not be feasible, but keep the structure of the house in mind. Get professional advice from an architect, a structural engineer, or a qualified building contractor before you make any final decisions. The person whom you consult should visit your house and should also check the original blueprints, if available, before approving any structural changes.

KITCHEN SURVEY

*I*t may be possible to design a new kitchen in a vacuum, but it is much easier to start with what you have and use it as a springboard for a new design. Whether you are designing alone or with professional help, begin the kitchen survey while you gather new ideas from other sources.

Start the survey by thinking through the primary activities that take place in your kitchen. List the major problems that occur during each activity. Look at the basic layout of the kitchen; check the traffic patterns within the room and between the kitchen and related rooms; consider the counter and storage space and how they affect food storage, preparation, eating, and cleanup. Your goal at this stage is to determine how your kitchen works, or does not work, for you.

The second step is to examine all the elements of the existing room. Consider the hidden elements—the structure and utilities, the surface treatments, and the appliances and furnishings, and decide what you want to retain and what you want to eliminate.

At some point before you design the new kitchen you will need an accurate floor plan and elevation sketches of the present kitchen. Draw a base plan while you do the survey. This gives you a chance to put the kitchen into a two-dimensional form, which will help you to understand relative distances and relationships. The base plan also serves as a tool for making notes and gives you a chance to verify critical dimensions as you go over the kitchen. The feature on page 13 contains information on drawing plans.

Basic Layout

Kitchen layout is made up of three factors: the shape of the room formed by the walls, doorways, and windows; the size of the major elements in the room; and the relationships among all of these features.

Measure the length of each wall and note the placement of the doors and windows. Look for any hidden spaces that can be incorporated into the kitchen—nearby closets, pantries, utility rooms, and the spaces under stairways. Note everything that is on the other side of every kitchen wall. Don't forget to measure the height of the ceiling. Notice what type of ceiling you have and find out what is between the ceiling and the roof.

Take stock of all the built-in features in the room: the size of doors and windows, the placement of islands and peninsulas, and the size and configuration of wall cabinets and built-in appliances.

Measure the distances between different features in the kitchen. The work triangle formed by the three major fixtures—sink, cooktop, and refrigerator—is the basis of a good kitchen layout. For top efficiency, the recommended maximum distance is 4 to 7 feet on each side of the triangle, for a total of 12 to 21 feet. These days the configuration should also include the distance between the refrigerator and the microwave and between the sink and the wall oven, although they are used less frequently and can be located outside the basic work triangle. Consider how closely the existing kitchen corresponds to this ideal.

Making the most of a small area is a design goal of many kitchen remodelers. A mirrored back splash increases the visual space in this little room. The double-stripe inlay in the solid surface material countertop effectively lengthens the horizontal plane as well.

Observe an everyday activity, such as making and serving coffee, toast, or tea, and note any wasted motions or awkward steps. Think how the basic layout could be changed to make this activity more efficient.

Views are an important part of the basic layout of a kitchen. Note the views beyond the room and those within the room. Don't let the current location of a window limit the possibilities; windows can be moved. Go outdoors and see what you can see outside the kitchen.

Take special note of sight lines into the kitchen from other rooms. Check what you see from the eating area of the dining room. Do you like to look at dirty dishes while you eat? Walk into the kitchen. What is the first thing that you see? Does this view reflect what you want it to?

Traffic Patterns

Determining the pattern of traffic through the existing kitchen will help you to make the new kitchen more efficient. You must figure out how people move within the kitchen, and between the kitchen and related areas of the house. Observe people moving through the room. Check the access from outdoors and from other rooms and ask yourself whether every doorway is necessary. Must people and pets cut through the work triangle in order to pass through the kitchen? Pretend that you are putting away groceries. Is there a place to set down the grocery bag?

Pay attention to what happens when friends come over. Note the spots in the kitchen where people naturally tend to congregate.

Count the number of steps you take while performing a basic task, such as making breakfast or fixing school lunches. Measure the distance between the oven and the eating area and between the eating area and the cleanup area. If you find that you are doing more walking than working, assess the layout and identify the major problems.

Drawing a Base Plan

Sooner or later you will need accurate floor plans and elevations, both of the existing space and of the new design. To make these plans you will need some inexpensive materials that are easy to find in hardware, stationery, or art supply stores. These include a tape measure, a ruler or a T square, ¼-inch graph paper (that is, graph paper with four squares to the inch), pencils, an eraser, tracing paper, masking tape, a plastic right triangle, a compass, and a plastic template of kitchen elements (this last is optional).

To make a floor plan of the existing kitchen, start by sketching a rough plan—it does not have to be accurate—on which to record field measurements. Then measure and record such features as the overall dimensions of the kitchen; the dimensions of adjacent areas that the kitchen might expand into; the length of the wall space between windows, doors, and corners (measure to the window and doorjambs, not to the edge of the trim); the width of the windows and doors (jamb to jamb); the thickness of the walls; the width and depth of the cabinets and appliances; the location of the hot-air registers, plumbing hookups, electrical outlets, and telephone; the location of any steps or other changes in the floor height; the location of any significant overhead features, such as a skylight, low stairs, beams, or duct work; and the dimensions of the table and chairs. Take exact measurements, accurate within ⅛ inch, and record them in feet and inches.

Using the rough sketch and these measurements as a reference, draw a floor plan on graph paper at a scale of ½ inch (two squares) to one foot. Draw walls with two parallel lines, the distance between them indicating the thickness of the wall. Indicate windows with a third parallel line between the two wall lines. Show in which direction doors swing or slide. Use dashed lines for overhead beams and skylights. Use standard electrical symbols for lights, switches, and outlets.

After you have completed the floor plan, make elevation drawings of the walls. Use a separate sheet for each wall; label the sheets *north, south, east,* and *west.* You can use the floor plan dimensions to get started and complete the elevations by taking field measurements as you go. Don't bother with hardware and other fine details, except to experiment with options.

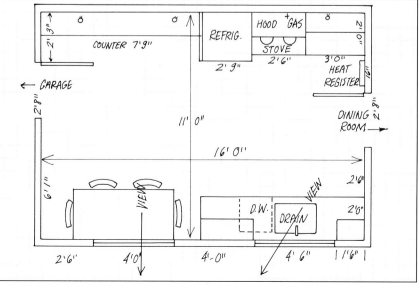

Counter Space

To survey the counter space, note the location and use of all the countertops. Measure the length, width, and height of every counter. Think about all the tasks that are performed at each. Consider everyone who uses the kitchen.

Are these counters efficient for your use? Are you trying to do everything on one small counter? Do youngsters draw or do their homework at the serving counter? Is there a place for dirty dishes beside the sink? A drainboard for clean ones? A place to chop? A place to lay out the plates when you are serving dinner? Where do you set down the groceries? Is counter space next to the refrigerator? Is it on the side that the refrigerator door opens to? Is there room to set down a hot pot next to the cooktop or the oven? Are the counters too high? Too low? Are different heights needed for different cooks? Can you sit at any of them? Do visitors congregate at one of the counters? List the areas where the biggest problems occur, where you want more counter space, and where the existing counter space is not used efficiently.

Storage

You may lack storage space simply because all the cabinets are full of items that rarely, if ever, get used. Start your storage survey by listing everything you find in the cabinets that you rarely use. Find places other than the kitchen to store these items.

Now concentrate on the storage spaces themselves. Measure the width and depth of each cabinet. Are they too shallow? Too deep? Are there items so far back in a cabinet that you've forgotten you even owned them?

Look for wasted space above and below the shelves. Are any shelves too high to reach? Too low? Are the shelves adjustable?

What is each storage area designed to contain? Are cooking utensils stored near the cooktop? Are spices and herbs organized neatly and stored in a convenient place? Are they stored where heat and light will quickly cause them to deteriorate, in open shelves, for example, above the range or sink? How convenient are the drawers for flatware and table accessories? Do you have any pantry or other storage space large enough to hold the biggest roasting pan? The 40-cup coffee urn? The picnic baskets and coolers?

If you recycle newspapers, cans, and bottles, there should be a convenient place where you can store these items temporarily.

Don't forget about cleaning implements and supplies. Is there a closet for the broom, mop, and vacuum? Is there a place for storing cleaning products safely out of a child's reach?

As you survey your storage needs, count how many drawers, shelves, bins, and closets you have and whether or not they are adequate.

Consider appearance as well as function. Note any storage units that are not sound and those that are so well built that you would hate to give them up. Consider open shelving and whether you have enough space for items that you would like to display.

Look at the soffit, the area above the wall cabinets. Sometimes the cabinets reach all the way to the ceiling. Other times the tops of the cabinets form an open shelf below the ceiling. Occasionally a wall is finished flush with the cabinet tops. Note whether the soffit is open or closed and consider which style you would prefer.

Above: Extra seating is cleverly stored underneath the center island in this modern-style gourmet kitchen.
Opposite: When this house was built utility rooms were common. Today's needs are different. Demolishing the wall between the kitchen and the utility room—about where the refrigerator is located—provided space for a pantry and a breakfast nook.

Hidden Elements

The hidden elements consist of all the parts of the kitchen that are not visible to the naked eye. You need to understand how the room is built in order to know exactly what kind of changes you can make. Get professional advice for an addition or for major interior changes, but use the following guidelines to survey as much as possible.

Walls

Most houses are framed with 2 by 4s and covered with wallboard, lath and plaster, or with wood paneling on the inside and exterior siding on the outside. Do not assume, however, that your walls are standard. Try to measure the thickness of each wall and verify the size of the interior framing members (2 by 4, 2 by 6, and so forth). The thickness of the wall is a critical factor in concealing drainpipes and vent pipes; in ordering new windows (you may need jamb extensions for thicker walls); in hanging heavy cabinets; and in matching new walls to old ones if you plan to extend them.

If you plan to remove or alter a wall, you must know whether it is a load-bearing wall—that is, whether it is part of the structure that holds the house together—or merely a partition wall. Treat exterior walls as bearing walls. If you can get access above the ceiling of an interior wall, note whether the joists run at right angles to or parallel to the wall in question. If they run at right angles, it is probably a bearing wall. Check also to see whether the exterior walls are insulated. Do they show any signs of leaks that should be corrected?

How high are the walls? Standard height is 8 feet, but do not assume that your walls are standard; always measure. Abnormal wall heights may affect the dimensions of the cabinets and soffits, the location of the overhead light fixtures, the size of the wall-finishing materials, and the framing techniques that you employ in making structural changes.

Ceilings

Notice the height and the construction of the ceiling and consider how these factors affect the kitchen design. Most kitchen ceilings are constructed with wood framing and finished with wallboard, lath and plaster, acoustical tile, or even asbestos products. Some ceilings are sloped, reflecting the pitch of the roof. Does the room feel cramped and dark because it has a low ceiling? Are there options? If you wish to raise the ceiling, is there attic space above it? Also, note which way the ceiling joists and rafters run. Their position will affect the wiring as well as any structural changes that you make. Look for insulation in the ceiling. What type of insulation is it, and is there enough?

Floors

You need to inspect the finish floor, the subfloor, and the framing. Note the condition of all the materials involved. The existing floor covering has little effect on your remodeling choices, but whether or not the floor is sound is a key factor. If the floor squeaks, if it slopes, or if you find damp or rotted areas, have the floor inspected from below. These problems must be corrected during construction. Check the framing to make sure that it is strong enough to withstand the addition of new major appliances or the extra weight of a new ceramic-tile finish floor or granite countertop.

Plumbing

Verify the locations and positions of the existing water and gas lines. Check the roof or attic to locate the sink vent. Check under the floor for the sink drain and the main house drain. Take accurate measurements to determine exact locations. If you plan to move the sink, make sure that there is enough clearance beneath the floor joists to extend the horizontal drain upstream and still maintain a proper slope. Look for cleanouts or other fittings that can be tapped into.

Note the inside diameter of the sink drainpipe. If it is only 1½ inches, you will have to upsize it to 2 inches if you are installing a dishwasher. If you are installing a washing machine, codes may require a 3-inch branch drain for the whole kitchen. Locate the water heater and hot-water pipes that serve the kitchen. Find out whether the pipes are insulated.

Wiring

The electrical system in many older homes cannot carry the load of today's appliances. Many of these require their own circuit. A properly wired kitchen may have eight or more circuits for the various appliances, outlets, and light fixtures.

Start your survey at the main service entrance. Is the drop from the power pole the old two-wire type or are there three wires, indicating that the system can carry 240-volt appliances? What is the amperage rating of the main breaker or fuse block? It should be at least 100 amps if a properly wired kitchen is to be added to the house load. If it is less than 100 amps you should consider having a new service entrance installed before or during the remodeling. If the circuit breakers are labeled, list the ones that serve appliances, outlets, or lights in the kitchen. Compare your list with the one on page 82, which lists the typical circuits of a properly wired kitchen. Are there blank spaces in the panel for additional circuit breakers? Is the main breaker convenient to the kitchen? If not, and if several circuits must be added, it might be easier to install a new subpanel closer to the kitchen.

Locate all the kitchen outlets and see whether they are grounded. Lights should be on a separate circuit from outlets; if they are not, the wiring must be altered during construction. If the stove is a gas model, is there a 120-volt electrical outlet behind it for accessories?

Finally, consider areas of the room where an extra electrical outlet would come in handy. Plan to install these during remodeling.

Heating and Cooling

If you are satisfied with the present heating and cooling system, just note the locations of the ducts, registers, radiators, and other outlets. If you are not satisfied with the present system and will be opening up walls, now is the time to plan changes. For a hot-water system consider replacing outdated radiators with modern baseboards. For a forced-air system consider installing a register in the toe kick under the sink cabinet to provide warmth where it's needed. Seek professional advice for any changes.

Energy Efficiency

As you survey the present kitchen and design a new one, think about all the ways that energy can be conserved. Is the insulation up to local standards? Do the windows and doors have weather stripping? Is it possible to install south-facing windows that will let in the winter sun for added warmth? Can the heating system be zoned to prevent unnecessary heat from entering the kitchen when cooking and baking have already made it warm? Is the kitchen exposed to the hot afternoon sun, adding to the cooling load during the time when dinner is being prepared? Are the windows and skylight all of the insulating type?

Don't forget the energy efficiency of your appliances. Are they in fact rated for energy efficiency? Does the refrigerator have a power saver switch or a humid-dry switch for turning off a heating element designed to remove external condensation? Does the dishwasher have a built-in water heater, allowing the house water heater to be turned down? Does it have an automatic air-drying cycle? Does the gas range have pilotless electronic ignition? Does the oven have a window? Do you have a microwave oven to reduce the use of the conventional oven? Are the light fixtures fluorescent?

Lighting

Lighting affects the efficiency and ambience of a kitchen. When you survey the existing lighting, take into account all forms of natural and artificial light. Where is the sun in relation to the kitchen at various times of the day? At various times of the year? Is there a way to take better advantage of the natural light? Note harsh shadows formed by permanent fixtures and sight lines directly facing windows, where glare may be a problem.

Sources of artifical light are easily identified. Note the type and location of each fixture. Indicate whether the light is fixed or on rheostats (dimmer switches). Consider whether the light is harsh or warm and whether it is suitable for all of your needs. Look for places where more light would be welcome. Note any shadows formed by ceiling fixtures. Indicate the location of each switch, and look for places where an extra switch might come in handy. Remember that if you plan to change the lighting you will probably be required to bring it up to code. This often entails the use of energy efficient fixtures, such as fluorescent tubes.

Finish Treatments

Although you will want to choose finish treatments on the basis of style and color, you should consider the practical aspects as well. Remember to consider all the major surfaces in relation to one another. If you replace one surface, you may want to replace others to match.

Make a list of the basic style elements in the present kitchen—color and texture of wallcoverings and floors, color and style of cabinets, countertop materials, and window treatment. Use this list to help you to determine what creates the overall look of the room. Do you like that look? Does the kitchen have a particular style? Do you like the present color scheme?

Look for a focal point in the present kitchen. Is it attractive? Are there design assets that you want to preserve, such as pleasant views, access to a garden, an interesting ceiling or wall, attractive moldings or hardware, or exposed beams? Are there liabilities, such as columns, pipes, undesirable views, or awkward angles?

Consider the details as well. Is it the cabinets themselves that you don't like, or would new handles give them, and the room, an entire new look? Do the accessories pull the room together or simply fill the space? Do you have room to display colorful towels, copper pots and pans, and other *batterie de cuisine*?

Appliances and Furnishings

List all the present major appliances and furnishings, noting the type, size, color, style, and age of each. This list should include the sink or sinks; the range, cooktop, or oven; the refrigerator; the dishwasher; the garbage disposer; the trash compactor; the table and chairs; and any other large furniture that you keep in the kitchen.

Now decide what to do with each item. Make three columns to the right of the list; label them *keep, replace, rejuvenate*. First ask yourself whether the item is sound. Then consider whether it fills your needs.

Next ask yourself whether each item is the style and color that you prefer. Do all the major appliances match? Do you like the color?

Consider rejuvenating appliances. Repainting or refinishing existing appliances and furniture is an excellent way to save money on a remodeling project. However, you need to be sure that each appliance will be useful in the new kitchen. Before you decide whether to keep, replace, or rejuvenate each item, you should perform a life-style inventory.

LIFE-STYLE INVENTORY

T*he checklists in this section will help you to focus on your family's living patterns and personal needs as they relate to the kitchen.*

Some questions suggest specific features that you may want to include in your kitchen; some give you criteria for designing the basic elements; and some help you to define the overall style.

Determining your life-style needs is not a test, nor is it something to be completed in one sitting. Doing this inventory is a process that may take several sessions. Get as many family members as possible to help fill out the questionnaire, so that everyone who uses the kitchen can contribute to the project.

Cooking Habits
□ How many people cook at once?
□ Is anyone left-handed?
□ Is it difficult for the cook to bend over? Reach high?
□ Do you prefer informal living, with the activities centered in the kitchen?
□ Does anyone need wheelchair access?
□ Do you bake often enough to require a separate baking center?
□ Do you engage in seasonal activities, such as canning, that require special equipment or extra space?
□ Do you freeze quantities of food?
□ Do you recycle?
□ Where do you like to keep the cookbooks?
□ When do you wash cooking utensils and dishes—after the meal or as you go along?
□ Do you store wine in the kitchen?
□ Do you store dried foods or bulk foods in the kitchen?
□ Are you constantly collecting new cooking gadgets?

Eating Habits
□ Does everyone eat meals together, or at separate times?
□ Do you prefer an intimate area for dining, or an open floor plan?
□ Do you desire morning sunshine at breakfast time?
□ Do you eat outside often?
□ Do you have several sets of dishes that take up a lot of storage space?
□ Do pets eat in the kitchen?

Home Environment
□ Do you watch television in the kitchen?
□ Do you do laundry in the kitchen?
□ Do you want a home office in the kitchen?
□ Do you use the kitchen for gardening chores, such as potting plants?
□ Does your house have a distinctive architectural style to maintain?
□ Does anyone see the kitchen as his or her own private retreat?
□ Do you want art in the kitchen?

Magnolia the dog comes running when she hears her pet-food drawer opening. Don't forget the unique needs of your own family when you design your cabinets. This narrow drawer next to the sink is specially designed to hold pounds of dry dog food.

Children

☐ Will you be supervising children while you cook?
☐ Do you want children to have access to counter space—either special low counters just for them or hidden steps to enable them to reach the regular counters?
☐ Can you see out-of-door play areas from the kitchen?
☐ Will the kitchen be used for homework and other projects?

Entertaining

☐ Do you serve formal dinners?
☐ Do you like guests to come into the kitchen?
☐ Do you entertain outdoors?
☐ Do you want more than one oven?

Future Changes

☐ Will you have a new baby; a son, daughter, niece, or nephew returning from school or the service; or an elderly parent living with you soon?
☐ Will anyone in the family soon be leaving home?
☐ Do you plan to stay in your home after you retire?
☐ Are you interested in resale?

Setting Goals

Review your notes from the kitchen survey and the life-style inventory and establish priorities. First list the most critical problems—the things that must be changed. Rank them in approximate order of importance. Then list the things that you would like to change. Finally, list the things that you could do without but that it would be nice to have.

You may modify this priority list as you continue the design process and begin to see trade-offs. Clarifying your priorities is a very important step in developing your new floor plans.

Developing Preliminary Plans

The base plan and the elevations of the present kitchen form the basis for new sketches and new ideas. These are developed in a series of preliminary plans. To get started, lay tracing paper over the base plan and draw the perimeter walls and other permanent features. Make several photocopies of the tracing so that you'll have plenty of extras on which to try out different configurations.

Now is the time to fit all the elements you want to have in the new kitchen into whatever space is allowed by the permanent features of the room. Loosely sketch in different activity centers, traffic patterns, and sight lines.

Consider the work triangle and its location in relation to the eating area. Locate the other major appliances, the cabinets, and the countertops. Sketch in the windows and doors. Experiment. Don't worry about taking exact measurements at this stage. What is important here is creativity.

The activity areas must also be compatible with the information covered on the base plan. The fixtures and appliances should be located near the appropriate utility lines. (The sink, dishwasher, and garbage disposer should also be located near a drain line.) It is usually possible to move these utilities—but it does add to the cost of the remodeling project.

Remember that the kitchen design will be very strongly influenced by the shape of the existing features. Relate the forms and lines of the new features to the forms and lines that are already present in the room. Play with the angles, widths, and heights of various elements.

Make notes on your drawings to help you to keep track of your ideas. Use arrows to indicate relationships between areas, and traffic patterns within the kitchen and between the kitchen and related rooms.

Don't stop as soon as you find one solution to a problem. Instead, develop several different preliminary plans and compare the advantages and disadvantages of each. Doing this will open you up to new ideas. To speed the process, cut out cardboard templates of the basic fixtures and appliances and move them around on an open base plan to see how different layouts work.

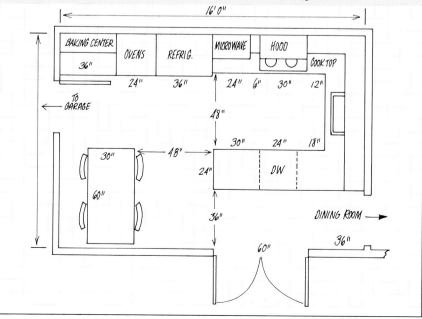

DESIGN PRINCIPLES

Properly designed kitchens not only function well but also look beautiful. Create a strong sense of harmony and balance by considering the basic elements of all design: line, form, scale, pattern, texture, and color. Weigh each principle when you plan the features, select the fixtures, and choose the finishes.

Line

As a visual element line contributes to the overall feeling of a kitchen. Strong horizontal lines emphasize serenity and also make a kitchen feel contemporary. Vertical lines emphasize formality and a traditional style. A narrow room will feel wider if lines cross the narrow dimension. You can achieve this effect by putting beams on the ceiling or a soffit across the top of the narrow end wall. Diagonal lines add drama and movement, while curves add elegance and grace.

Study the vertical and horizontal lines formed by the edges and corners of the countertops, doors, cabinets, windows, appliances, and other features of the existing kitchen. Look for ways to smooth them out so that they align better with one another. Are the edges and doors of the wall cabinets aligned with those of the base cabinets? Are the oven doors aligned with any other feature? Is the top of a doorway aligned with any cabinets or shelves? Would extending the wall cabinets to the ceiling help the overall look? You may not be able to move all these features into perfect alignment, but make as many adjustments as possible.

When you choose cabinets and countertop details, consider the visual impact of lines. A plain face will accentuate the edges and seams of a cabinet. Cabinets with horizontal slats will elongate the kitchen. Vertical patterns will draw the eye upward. Countertop edges that contrast with the cabinets will create strong lines; countertops trimmed to match the cabinets (with a wood strip, for instance) will tend to mask the line.

Form

The principle of form relates to the shape and mass of the various elements in the design. Simply put, continuity in form lends harmony to a design. Certain forms have deep-seated symbolic connotations. Vertical forms induce a sense of awe. Diminutive and intricate forms tend to evoke curiosity and interest. A horizontal plane promotes feelings of peacefulness. Forms made up of straight lines are an expression of reason. Circular forms give a feeling of closure. Curves symbolize harmony. Projecting and jagged forms suggest dynamism and may imply speed, strength, and power.

Rectangular forms dominate most kitchens. In order to be harmonious, however, they must have similar proportions. Look at the shapes of the doors, windows, cabinets, island, appliances, and so forth. Do they all repeat a similar form, or do they clash? Unique shapes—a curved window or an archway, for instance—should be repeated elsewhere in the kitchen or in related rooms to tie the design together.

Scale

An expression of relative size, scale refers to the relationships among the various elements of the room. Properly scaled spaces relate well to the people using them. When considering the proper scale for the kitchen, consider the size of the room and the size of the various objects within the room.

Are all the objects in the kitchen in scale with one another and with the room as a whole? If the room is large consider scaling the cabinets slightly larger, buying the largest sink available, and choosing a thick edge detail for the countertops to keep everything in balance.

By the same token, scale down the features of a small kitchen. Choose slightly smaller appliances and consider small patterns in tile, wallcovering, and window treatments. This does not mean that everything in the room should be diminutive, just in scale.

Pattern

The ordered regularity of the elements in a design is called a pattern. These are created by the print on tiles and wallcoverings, by the grain of the wood on cabinets and furnishings, by the shape of drawer pulls and handles, and by the grid of floor covering and countertop material.

In most kitchens the goal is to strike a balance between too much of the same pattern, and too many different patterns vying for attention. One approach is to reduce pattern to a bare minimum by using plain materials, such as laminates and painted wallboard, throughout the design. Another approach is to repeat the same pattern in several finishes, matching, for instance, wallcoverings, window coverings, and tiles.

Yet another approach is to use materials with random patterns, such as flat-grained wood cabinets, wall coverings with floral designs, open displays of cookware, and plants, and to coordinate them by matching the textures and colors.

Texture

Study the visual and tactile surface of all the materials used in the kitchen. Most kitchen textures are smooth, because they are durable and easy to maintain, but smooth surfaces are not all alike. Polished wood looks and feels different from laminate. Glazed tile has a texture very different from that of stainless steel.

The same smooth material may even come in a choice of textures, such as a glossy or a matte version of the same plastic laminate. Consider texture when you select all your materials. Do you want the kitchen to feel like something out of an auto body shop, all sleek and shiny? Or do you prefer matte finishes, to give it that earthy feeling?

Color

A powerful design element, color is not an afterthought or a decoration but a force in its own right that transforms space and gives it character.

A helpful device for choosing a color scheme is a color wheel, sold at art supply stores, which looks like a rainbow pie cut into 12 segments. The primary colors—red, blue, and yellow—are equidistant from one another. Each of the secondary colors—green, orange, and violet—is placed halfway between the two primary colors that are its components. The remaining six segments are tertiary colors, created by blending one primary with one secondary color. They are red-orange, red-violet, blue-violet, blue-green, yellow-green, and yellow-orange.

Harmonious color schemes can be created by combining colors from the wheel in various ways. Choosing one or more intensities from the same segment produces a monochromatic scheme. Choosing colors from opposite sides of the wheel forms a complementary scheme.

To produce a simple triad scheme, take colors from three segments spaced equidistantly. Another three-color scheme, called split complementary, is produced by taking one color from one segment and the other two colors from segments on each side of the segment opposite the first. Choosing colors from two or more contiguous segments creates an analogous, or related, color scheme. A quadratic scheme consists of colors from any four segments, as long as no two segments are adjacent.

Where do you start? If there are permanent materials already in the kitchen start with that color and build a scheme around it; begin with the color of a cabinet or a countertop or with the colors in an adjacent room. You can also build a color scheme around a fabric, wallcovering, or a painting.

Also consider the physical effects that colors produce. Reds, oranges, and yellows are warm; blues, greens, and violets are cool. Colors also have emotional values. Blue aids concentration. Green is peaceful and soothing. Red is stimulating.

You can use color to alter the spatial characteristics of the room. If the kitchen is small, use light colors to make it feel more spacious. If the ceiling is low, a light color will cause it to recede. If it is high and makes the kitchen feel too formal, use dark colors on the floor and countertops to create a more intimate feeling. Make a long, narrow kitchen feel wider by using light colors on the long walls and a dark color on the short end wall. Use intense colors to make certain features stand out or muted colors to play them down.

Color, especially dramatic color, must be carefully planned for effective results.

CHOOSING A KITCHEN STYLE

*T*oo often kitchens are designed by choosing the separate components and then hoping that they all work together. Avoid this haphazard approach by choosing an overall kitchen style and theme to guide your design.

You will probably get a pretty good idea of what you want as you collect ideas and survey your own kitchen, although you may not know how to describe it or know what gives it that certain flavor. The architecture of your home and the kitchen space itself may also suggest a certain style, although nearly every kitchen theme can be developed in nearly every type of home.

We have divided kitchens into two broad categories—traditional and modern. Choose one of these two categories to determine how you want the kitchen to *feel*. Later, when you pick the kitchen theme, you'll be determining how you want it to *look*. Once you identify the basic characteristics of each style, you will get a better idea of what you want for your own kitchen.

Traditional

A traditional kitchen can be stately and formal or busy and ornate. The emphasis is on vertical lines; classic, timeless materials, such as marble and fine wood; and a sense of order and decorum. Details are refined, displays restrained. Window areas are limited; this kitchen has an inward orientation.

Everything in the room suggests old-world craftsmanship and elegance. Natural materials and fibers dominate. Patterns are small; materials have texture; and colors are muted and subdued.

Modern

Modern kitchens range from formal to casual, but they have in common clean lines and smooth surfaces. The emphasis is on the horizontal line with occasional angles and curves.

Colors are bold and intense, either monochromatic or tending toward high contrast. Materials are modern, and artificial rather than natural; they include glass block, chrome, laminates, and stainless steel. Patterns are strong, often geometric.

There is no inessential trim in modern kitchens. Windows, open shelves, and accessories are arranged in geometric, balanced forms.

A modern kitchen needn't be stark. The color and style of furnishings and accessories coordinate this cozy breakfast nook to both the kitchen next to it and the deck outside.

Kitchen Themes

The second step in determining style is to choose an appropriate kitchen theme. The end result will be a well-defined room—traditional or modern, with a personality: country, southwestern, neoclassical, art deco. Most kitchen themes are vernacular. They reflect the characteristics of a period, a place, or an architectural style. A kitchen rarely falls into a single category that can be described in a few words. The descriptions that follow provide a vocabulary of attributes to work with so that you can develop a theme for your kitchen. This is by no means an inclusive list, just a few ideas for you to use.

Art Deco

Geometric and sensuous, the art deco kitchen has the look of a 1950s diner. High-contrast basic colors, such as black and white, pink and black, or dark green and yellow, recreate the mood. Plain painted wood or metal cabinets with chrome trim, laminate countertops, and checkered resilient floor tiles all work well. An old or reproduction dinette set would complete the look.

Classic

A classic kitchen is one that shows off the beauty of handsome materials and accessories. Cabinets are framed with raised-panel designs and are built to the ceiling. Sometimes they are made of rich woods, such as cherry or pecan, and stained or color-washed in shades of blue, gray, or green. Sometimes they are painted white without contrasting wood trim or details.

Walls are most often papered; windows are edged and trimmed with moldings and hung with curtains. Hardwood, ceramic tile, and plain resilient flooring work well in a classic setting. Fine art, fine china, and displayed brass or copper cookware are appropriate accessories.

Contemporary

Contemporary kitchens have a sleek air about them. They are devoid of clutter; walls, countertops, and cabinet fronts are bare. Cabinets are usually frameless, often finished in laminate with a contrasting trim.

Countertops are of slab stone, solid surface materials, glazed undecorated tile, or stainless steel. They should be highly polished. Mirrored back splashes add to the sleek feel.

Windows are not trimmed and are left uncovered whenever possible. Contemporary kitchens may contain artwork, but the frames should be simple. Kitchen equipment is tucked out of sight into appliance garages, in keeping with the look of clean, wide-open spaces.

American Country

Casual and informal, American country kitchens tend toward the rustic with a warm, exuberant feeling. They feature frame cabinets, usually made out of oak or pine, in warm tones or sometimes frosted or painted white. Windows with many small panes create an old-fashioned look. Stained glass windows work well; other windows are hung with curtains. Countertops in neutral tones with wood trim evoke the country feeling. Wallcoverings with small floral or subtle repetitive patterns work well. Choose pendant lighting. Accessories include favorite antiques.

French Country

The French country kitchen is an unpretentious room, full of charm but more refined than rustic. Consider ceramic tile for floors and countertops and decorated tile for back splashes. The suggestion of stone or plaster walls evokes an old-world charm. Fruitwood or white cabinets have simple brass hardware. Window treatments feature fabrics, usually checks or paisleys. Detailing is simple and elegant throughout.

Euro-Style

This futuristic theme emphasizes function, lack of clutter, and easy maintenance. Lines are uninterrupted and sleek. These kitchens are efficient and have a compact, crisp feeling; this theme is an excellent choice for a small room.

Colors can be bright but the design is monochromatic with subtle accents. Patterns, other than a simple grid on floors or countertops, should be avoided.

Frameless cabinets are an essential element of the Euro-style; they are covered in laminates or wood veneers. Appliances are scaled down and compact. Often they are integrated with the cabinet system.

Counters are slab or dimensioned stone, laminate, or solid-surface material. Floors should be uniform in color. Windows are best left uncovered; if this is impossible, the coverings should blend in with the walls. Accessories should have a sculptural feeling.

Gourmet

For the serious cook, a theme that emphasizes food storage and preparation is ideal. Appliances tend to be commercial models. Heavy-duty, industrial shelving and stainless steel and butcher-block countertops work well. A menu-planning area is a must.

Neoclassical

Materials that suggest Greek and Roman architecture characterize the neoclassical theme. Often these materials are used with a certain amount of whimsy. Suggest classical forms with columns and pediments. Use paint to create stone finishes.

Southwestern

Rustic and casual with an open feel, the southwestern theme uses pastel colors, especially peach, teal, and turquoise. This kitchen must be sunny and well lit. Consider pine cabinets; ceramic tile floors; and textured plaster walls and ceilings. Regional artifacts make good accessories.

DESIGNING THE NEW KITCHEN

*A*fter looking at other kitchens, surveying the existing room, setting lifestyle priorities, and developing a kitchen style, you'll want to get down to the details of designing the new kitchen. The goal is to blend the realities of budget, space, and structure with the possibilities suggested by your priority list to produce a beautiful kitchen that works well.

Designing your new kitchen is a juggling act. You can work on only one or two variables at a time, keeping the others suspended in the air. This can be fun and exhilarating, and it can be frustrating. Be patient. Get help. And don't be surprised if you have to start over several times.

You may find that at first you have difficulty seeing the existing kitchen in new ways. Try not to be timid, making only slight modifications. If necessary, start with a blank sheet of paper and—forgetting about the budget—create layouts that include anything and everything you ever wanted in a kitchen. This may sound like a waste of time, but it fires your imagination and sparks creative solutions. Besides, it's fun.

Opposite: Save steps and time during food preparation by laying out the sink, cooktop, and refrigerator in a work triangle. This triangle is the basis of a well-designed kitchen. Wood panels, designed to match the cabinet fronts, hide the refrigerator on the far wall.

Basic Design Guidelines

The designer's first goal is to create the most efficient work space possible. The following guidelines will help you to get started. Review them several times—many ideas overlap and must be considered simultaneously. Keep in mind that not everyone has the same cooking style and storage needs. Adapt these principles to your own situation; don't treat them as rigid formulas.

Enlarging the Space

If one of your goals is to enlarge the existing kitchen, look at your base plan and try to find ways to expand. Consider all the spaces surrounding the kitchen. Do these spaces offer possiblities for expansion?

Even if you have no room (or budget) to expand, there may be ways to make the kitchen feel larger. Look for an activity center, such as the laundry, that could be moved elsewhere. Think about installing a garden window over the counter to bring in more of the outdoors, extend the countertop visually, and provide extra shelves for potted plants that would otherwise be kept on the counter. Open the ceiling to the pitched roof to give a greater sense of space without increasing the floor area. Install a bay window with a window seat to enlarge a small dining alcove. Moving a door or eliminating it to solve a traffic problem may also create enough new wall area to solve a space problem. Exchanging a table and chairs for a built-in counter often adds much-needed space.

The Work Triangle

Most kitchen activity takes place in the space between the sink, the cooktop, and the refrigerator. This arrangement is generally referred to as the work triangle. The most efficient kitchen designs place the triangle apart from traffic areas. The main appliances should be close enough together to save steps but far enough apart to allow for adequate work space and storage space. Strive for a distance of 5 to 7 feet between the refrigerator and the sink, 4 to 6 feet between the sink and the cooktop, and 5 to 9 feet between the cooktop and the refrigerator. Ideally, the combined distances should total no less than 4 feet and no more than 22 feet.

A U- or L-shaped kitchen with an island allows for the most efficient work triangle. A kitchen confined to one wall or a galley kitchen with a corridor running through it is the least efficient.

Placement of the sink depends on the plumbing. You may be able to move the sink 3 or 4 feet from its present location without having to make major changes in the water line. Locating the sink against a bathroom wall or near the laundry may also save on the plumbing work. The cooktop generally requires an overhead hood or down-draft ventilating system, so it should be placed where the duct work can be run to the outside.

Consider the location of the appliances in relation to the windows. A window over the sink will allow you to take a pleasant break from staring at dirty dishes, but a window over the cooktop is a safety hazard. Drafts could extinguish the gas burners, billowing curtains could ignite, and if you reached over the cooktop to open or close the window, you could get burned.

The relationship between the sink and the cooktop depends on your cooking habits. If you tend to work with dripping pots of water or wet hands, place the two appliances where they can be connected by a countertop. Don't place them at opposite sides of an open floor.

Don't worry if you can't fit a wall oven, dishwasher, separate freezer, or barbecue grill into the work triangle. These appliances take up valuable space. They can go outside the triangle in separate work centers.

The Cleanup Center

Plan a cleanup center around the sink leg of the triangle, unless you have the space and budget for a second sink near the eating area. For planning purposes figure the width of a double-bowl sink as 36 inches and the width of a single-bowl sink as 24 inches. Provide at least 24 inches of counter on one side for stacking dirty dishes and 18 to 30 inches on the other side for draining clean dishes. For corner locations, the sink should be at least 9 inches from the intersection of the two counters or set at an angle, so that there is elbowroom on both sides.

Locate the dishwasher close to the sink, on the side away from the work triangle. Allow a space 24 inches wide below the counter. For tight spaces, consider an 18-inch model or a special model that can be installed under the sink. The dishwasher door should not interfere with adjacent cabinets or appliances. Make sure that there is room to stand at the sink when the dishwasher door is open. Plan storage for everyday dishes and flatware close to the dishwasher.

The garbage container should be near the food preparation area. Consider a trash compactor, a pull-out or tilt-out receptacle built into a base cabinet, a container mounted on a sink door, a countertop hatch, or (if space permits) a freestanding container. Whatever your choice, make it easily accessible; you will often need to get to this container when both hands are occupied. Consider installing separate bins for recycling.

Towels must be handy. If you like to display them, provide a towel bar at the end of a convenient cabinet. For concealed storage, consider a pull-out rack under the sink or in a special base cabinet, or a bar mounted inside a convenient pantry door.

Scrubbers and sponges can be concealed in a tilt-out tray built into the sink base, a feature offered by most cabinet lines.

If you enjoy formal dining, make sure that the cleanup area cannot be seen from the eating area.

The Food Preparation Center

Most food preparation takes place in the area between the refrigerator and the sink and in the area around the cooktop. Consider how you move within and between these areas when you plan it. Provide 36 to 42 inches of counter for general food preparation. The cooktop should have at least 21 inches of working counter on one side and at least 12 inches on the other side in order to accommodate pot handles safely. Part, if not all, of the countertop should be covered with heat-resistant material. The cooktop should not be crowded against a sidewall, and it should be at least 9 inches away from any corner where two counters intersect, so that you won't have to lean over the cooktop to reach into the corner.

When looking for a microwave oven, consider what size you want, which way its door opens, whether you want a built-in or a countertop model, and how much counter space you have. Provide at least 15 inches of counter below the microwave or next to it on the latch side. The door should swing away from the work area. Don't put the microwave in a

Open doors reveal a bustling laundry center at one end of this traditional-style contemporary kitchen. An ironing board cupboard contains a pull-out "to be ironed" basket and an electrical outlet for plugging in the iron. The side-by-side washer and dryer allow for a wide countertop that makes a perfect folding table.

corner where the door cannot swing completely open. Don't put it lower than wrist height or higher than shoulder level. The ideal height is around elbow level.

A conventional oven should be accessible from the food preparation area, although it does not have to be within the work triangle. It may be part of a separate baking center.

If you do a lot of cooking, consider a sink for cleanup and another for food preparation, located between the refrigerator and the cooktop. Provide cutting boards, either built into the surface of the countertop or concealed, as pullouts.

To keep pots and pans within easy reach, consider an overhead rack, or deep drawers under the cooktop.

Provide shallow drawers near the cooktop for knives and pot holders.

Small appliances can be hidden in an appliance garage with a tambour or solid door to match the cabinets.

Extend the garage back through the wall if there is a closet or other dead space behind it, so that you have the full depth of the counter in front of the garage. Another way to conceal small appliances is to store them in a deep drawer beneath the countertop.

Provide handy storage for spices and condiments away from excessive heat and light, which may deteriorate some spices. Avoid placing them where you must reach over the cooking surface in order to get them. To free valuable cabinet space, consider installing a recessed spice shelf between the wall studs.

The Food Storage Center

In planning food storage, consider both the convenience of finding foods as you need them and the convenience of storing them quickly when you bring the groceries home. Allow a 33-inch to 36-inch space for

the refrigerator, if possible, even if the present model is not that wide. The doorswing should be such that you can reach into the refrigerator from the sink area. Plan at least 18 inches of counter on the latch side. Position refrigerator at the end of a counter rather than in the middle, where it would interrupt the flow of work. Make sure that one open door will not collide with open doors of other appliances. Consider an undercounter or apartment-sized model if space is tight.

Do you want the freezer to be part of the refrigerator or do you want it to be a separate unit? A full-sized separate unit could be placed outside the kitchen, in the pantry or garage. An undercounter model could go in the food preparation area.

Plan other food storage near the refrigerator, but not necessarily in the work triangle. Options include a walk-in pantry, a tall storage unit with built-in organizers, pull-out storage units, large corner cabinets, and drawers or bins for bulk items.

Consider special storage needs. Provide pull-out bins for produce that should not be stored in the refrigerator. In some climates you can revive the old-fashioned cooler with screened vents opening directly to a shady exterior wall. Wine should be stored at a constant 60° to 65° F, which is cooler than most kitchens. However, you may find a cool cabinet in a north corner of the kitchen, or consider installing an undercounter wine-cooler cabinet.

Finally, consider how you will store any miscellaneous items that do not fit into the work centers. These may include pet food, picnic equipment, brooms and mops, the tool kit, the fire extinguisher, aprons, gardening supplies, and ironing equipment.

Closed, the laundry center becomes an extra food preparation area and then triples as an elegant serving area for party buffets.

The Baking Center

A separate baking center allows you to bake frequently without interrupting other kitchen activities. Even if you don't have room for a separate center, incorporate as many of these features into the basic work area as you can. Plan at least 15 inches of counter space next to the oven and at least 36 inches of counter space nearby for mixing and preparation. This second counter should be lower than the others to make it easier to

Organizing the modern family is a job that deserves a desk of its own. Keep bills, address books, the family calendar, and recipes at your fingertips by integrating a communication center into your remodeled kitchen. Desks and shelves can be built to order or purchased ready-made from many cabinet manufacturers. Remember to include a telephone and one or more electrical outlets in the desk area.

roll out pastry, and consider a marble or stone countertop or insert.

To keep the countertop free of clutter while you work, plan a small shelf under the wall cabinets or a ledge along the back of the counter itself, if it happens to be extra deep. Provide convenient storage for mixing bowls and baking equipment. Trays, baking sheets, and muffin tins can be stored vertically in divided cabinets and baking pans can be kept in deep drawers. Large roasting pans that do not fit into the cooking area could also be stored in deep drawers. Keep measuring spoons and other utensils organized by hanging them on hooks, either along the back splash or inside the cabinet doors, or store them in shallow drawers with dividers.

The mixer and other appliances can be stored in a garage or deep drawer, or on a caddy. Provide an electrical outlet inside the cabinet. Organize storage for ingredients according to the size and type of the containers: bin drawers for bulk items, shelf space for boxes and packages, and a spice rack for small jars. Plan a holder for cookbooks, and a convenient shelf on which to store them. If there will be times when you will need extra counter space, plan a flip-up extension at the end of the countertop.

The Eating Area

When space permits, an eating area in the kitchen saves steps, creates an informal atmosphere, and lets you save the dining room for formal meals. Options include a separate table and chairs, a table with built-in banquette seating, a section of counter built at table height into a peninsula or island, or a work counter that doubles as an eating counter. The space between a table and wall should be at least 26 inches wide for seating and 36 to 44 inches wide if people must edge past a seated person. If the space serves as a passageway to another room, it should be at least 56 inches wide. The overhang for a breakfast bar

should be 15 to 18 inches deep, or 30 inches deep if there is seating on both sides.

Provide storage for serving pieces and table linens near the eating area. Dishes are stored here too, except for those everyday dishes that are stored in the cleanup area. Dishes can be stacked or displayed on narrow shelves where conventional counters or cabinets would take up too much room. You may also want to store certain small appliances, such as a toaster or coffee maker, near the eating area. Conceal them in a handy drawer or cabinet, and provide a special outlet so that they can be kept plugged in.

Communication Centers

A desk area some distance away from the work triangle can serve many needs. It can be a menu-planning center, a home office, a family communication center, or a homework center—so plan it well to keep the space organized and uncluttered. Make sure that it has the telephone lines and electrical outlets necessary for home office equipment. Provide shelves for cookbooks, magazines, personal objects, and study supplies. Plan drawers for family records, files, telephone books, writing materials, and computer supplies. Include a bulletin board or message center.

Many families enjoy watching television during certain meals or while preparing food and cleaning up. Consider the electrical and television cable lines, shelf space, and view lines when planning.

Every kitchen benefits from access to radio and stereo, so that you can listen to music while cooking and during parties. Wiring a set of speakers from the living room into the kitchen provides consistent sound throughout the house.

Today's home often requires a computer, a security-system center, an intercom, and a service panel for an outdoor irrigation system. Anticipate these present and future space and wiring needs when developing room allocations.

General Layout Hints

Provide at least 48 inches between appliances or counters that face each other. Try to avoid having two doors, such as those of an oven and a dishwasher, open toward each other. A U-shaped kitchen should have at least 60 inches, and ideally 72 inches, between the legs of the U to enable two cooks to work together comfortably. There should be at least 42 inches of clearance on all sides of an island or a peninsula. Put tall units, such as a refrigerator, wall oven, or pantry, at the end of a counter rather than in the middle. Corners must be carefully designed. Drawers and doors should not open into one another. Utilize the corner space with lazy-Susan units, or with swing-out or half-Susan shelves attached to a cabinet door.

When combining counters to form two adjacent work centers, use the larger size recommended for each use and add another 18 inches. Counters need not all be the standard 36 inches high. You can vary their height to accommodate different tasks and different cooks.

Integrate supporting posts or columns into a counter; don't leave them freestanding. Use them as a design element or conceal them in shelf units or utility chases. You can even integrate them into a communications kiosk complete with a message board and telephone.

Circulation and Access

As if planning an efficient work space were not involved enough, the new kitchen layout should also take into account the circulation patterns through the kitchen and access to the rest of the house. Will the new floor plan solve the circulation problems that you identified when you surveyed the existing room? Look at the main traffic corridors within and through the kitchen. Make sure that you will have convenient access to the dining room, the garage, and the front door.

The easiest way to assess the plan is to ask a series of ''What if'' questions. What if you are cooking and the doorbell rings? What if kids come into the kitchen from outdoors? What if you have a party and guests end up in the kitchen? What if you want to do the laundry while you cook? What if you are carrying two armloads of grocery bags in from the car? What if you want a midnight snack? What if you need to prepare dessert while the dirty dishes are being cleared from the table? What if the phone rings? As you ask yourself each question, plot the traffic pattern on the preliminary floor plan. See where the major traffic patterns develop, and look for ways to improve circulation.

Another important aspect of kitchen layout is relating the kitchen to the outdoors. Does the layout take advantage of the best views? Is it easy to serve food from the kitchen to the outdoor eating and entertaining areas? Can children playing outdoors be watched from the kitchen? Is there easy access to a kitchen garden or herb garden? Are there enough windows or skylights to provide adequate daylight? Do windows with a southern exposure maximize the potential for solar heat during the winter? Are there windows with an eastern exposure to capture the morning sun? Are west-facing windows shaded from the hot afternoon sun? If there are cabinets all along a wall, could windows be placed above them? Does the layout make it feasible to add a deck, a balcony, or a terrace in the future?

Safety Factors

Accidents in the kitchen are far too common. They happen especially to young children and to older adults. Safety conscious design and careful work habits reduce the chance of accidents. An efficient floor plan minimizes the need to twist, bend, and hurry—all actions that can lead to injury. These safety hints provide further protection against accidents.

□ Keep the main traffic paths away from the work area.
□ Provide a play space for toddlers nearby but not in the work area.
□ Keep the cooktop away from windows and doors that swing inward.
□ Provide counter space on both sides of the cooktop so that pot handles do not hang over the edge.
□ Avoid storing things where you have to reach over the cooktop to get to them.
□ Install a smoke alarm between the kitchen and the living areas.
□ Eliminate one-step changes in floor level.
□ Be sure that all floor areas and work surfaces are well lighted.
□ Keep a Class B:C fire extinguisher in or near the kitchen. It should not be next to the cooktop and it should be easily visible.
□ Protect all electrical outlets near the sink with ground fault circuit interrupter (GFCI) devices.
□ Provide enough electrical outlets to eliminate extension cords.
□ Provide separate storage for knives and keep them sharp.
□ Keep a first-aid kit in the kitchen.
□ Store large lids near the cooktop to use for smothering a grease fire.
□ Keep cleaning supplies and caustic chemicals in a separate cabinet with a childproof latch or lock.
□ Be sure that cooktop controls are childproof.
□ Get proper permits for all work done on the house.
□ Install appliances according to the manufacturers' instructions.
□ Know how to shut off the main gas valve to the house.

SPECIFYING MATERIALS AND EQUIPMENT

To choose cabinets, countertops, lighting, appliances, flooring, wall and ceiling treatments, and finishing details, you must weigh countless pros and cons. Each choice will affect your life at home for years to come. These choices are also the overriding factor in determining cost of the remodeling project. Use everything that you have learned up to this point to help you in your decision making.

Choosing Cabinets

It is hard to imagine a better storage system than built-in cabinets, or a kitchen remodeling that does not include them. A quick glance through the manufacturers' brochures or a trip to a kitchen showroom will reveal a stunning array of choices. When selecting cabinets you'll need to decide whether or not the cabinets should have frames; what material and color you prefer, and what size and type; and which storage options would serve you best.

Frame or Frameless

Face-frame cabinets have frames around the doors and drawers. Frameless cabinets have no face frames—only a thin crack between the doors and thin cracks between the drawer fronts. They are sometimes called Euro-style or full-overlay-style cabinets. The advantages of face-frame cabinets are a more traditional look, a more substantial feel, an emphasis on sculptural form, and less exacting installation. The advantages of frameless cabinets are more efficient storage features and the fact that they can be coordinated with certain appliance lines. They can cause problems in tight corners where doors cannot open fully and drawers cannot clear obstructions on the side, but filler pieces are available that will create enough clearance to solve these problems.

Materials and Colors

Another important choice when selecting cabinets is the type and color of the material used for the fronts and sides. The basic alternatives are wood, high-pressure laminate, or a combination of both, but there are innumerable variations of each. Wood can be solid or a thin veneer glued to plywood or pressed board. The grain pattern can be made up of open, swirly lines (sometimes called flat grain) or straight, parallel lines (usually called rift-sawn or vertical grain). Many kinds of wood are used for cabinets, each with its own unique characteristics. Oak, pine, ash, maple, and Douglas fir veneers have high-contrast grain patterns and tend to create an informal effect, although rift-sawn lumber and some types of maple look very formal. Pecan, birch, cherry, and walnut have more uniform, subtle patterns and tend to look rich and elegant. The style of construction also affects the appearance of wood. Solid-slab doors and drawer fronts, which have no edge trim, create a look of informal elegance and a contemporary mood. Fabricated fronts range from traditional "cathedral" styles to modern horizontal slats. Many styles evoke a specific historical period.

Finally, the choice of finish affects appearance. Wood can be stained or sealed to enhance its natural color and pattern; frosted or pickled to give it a uniform, clean feeling; or painted—usually white—with an enamel or epoxy finish to give flat-panel styles a contemporary look and raised-panel styles a traditional, country look.

Laminates are a popular choice for cabinets. The range of colors, patterns, and textures is immense, although white and almond are the big favorites. Many laminate cabinets have wood inlays or trim, which gives them a contemporary, Scandinavian look. Plain white laminate cabinets without trim tend to disappear into the background and can be worked into more traditional kitchen styles. They can be used in place of painted wood cabinets; laminates are less expensive and easier to maintain. Laminates also offer the option of bold colors, which can be mixed and matched to create a festive mood or coordinated with the countertops and flooring to create a monochromatic dreamscape—perhaps a serene, pastel desert, a deep blue grotto, or a sizzling red fantasy room.

Other variations in cabinet design that affect the appearance of the unit include glass doors; curved end units; and use of exotic materials and painted finishes.

Sizes and Types

As you refine the kitchen design you will need to consider the sizes and types of cabinets more carefully. Modular cabinets come in base, wall, and tall units. If you are buying ready-made modular cabinets, your choice of type and size will be limited to stock items. The more expensive custom factory lines offer a much wider selection. These manufacturers can also make special units to order. A local cabinet shop provides the most flexibility; it can tailor units to your unique requirements and offer a wide range of choices in hardware.

As you plan the sizes and types of cabinets, consider the following special situations. Choose corner units that make the best use of lost space. If you are considering buying a lazy-Susan unit, test it to see whether the door pinches your fingers when opening and closing and look for wasted space below the revolving shelves. For sink units, decide whether you want a full cabinet with sides and a floor, or a sink front, which must be carefully attached at the sides and for which you must build a floor on-site. Look for special cabinet units to hold wall ovens and microwaves. The space over the refrigerator is an ideal spot for a wall cabinet 24 inches deep (rather than the standard 12 inches). If there will be a wall cabinet over the sink, make it short enough to provide plenty of headroom. The short cabinets over the sink and the cooktop should align horizontally. Building codes will specify how close cabinets can be installed to cooktops. Don't stick a solitary wall cabinet in a corner next to a window or a door. Look for ways to consolidate it into the design, or seek another alternative.

Storage Options

Choose cabinets that utilize every square inch of space. Adjustable shelves eliminate dead space over stacks of dishes and boxes of food. Dividers make efficient use of space by keeping utensils, trays, pot lids, and spices organized. Pull-out wire racks allow you to see the utensils and stack them efficiently, but beware of the wasted space taken up by the racks themselves. Drawers beneath drop-in ranges, wall ovens, and even toe kicks utilize dead space. Deep drawers are more efficient than shelf units or pull-out units, but pull-out units make use of narrow spaces. A tilt-out tray makes use of the wasted space in front of the sink bowl.

Making a New Floor Plan

Once you have settled on one final preliminary plan, the last step of the design phase is to draw up a new floor plan, sometimes called a master plan. This plan will accurately show the shape and location of all the elements of the new kitchen.

Remember that you do not need to draw well to work out a floor plan. You are doing this only so that you can visualize your ideas. This final floor plan will also be helpful when you shop for materials, when you apply for permits, and when you are ready to begin the actual construction.

Using the preliminary plan as a reference, take a clean copy of the base plan tracing and block in the elements of your final design. Indicate the locations of the cabinets, countertops, and appliances and assign exact dimensions. Manufacturers' brochures give some standard dimensions. You might also visit the showrooms and retail outlets where you will be purchasing the products to make sure that your dimensions are accurate.

Although the characteristics of the materials that you choose will influence the form of the room, at this point you should concentrate on the shape of the space and on aesthetic relationships rather than on materials and construction.

It may be easier for you to visualize different shapes if you draw them to scale on separate pieces of paper. Then cut them out and lay them on the plan to see whether they appeal to you. When you develop a solution that you particularly like, trace it onto the plan.

Consider traffic patterns again during this stage. Double-check aisle widths, door widths, and the depth of countertops. Put as much detail into the floor plan as you feel you need. When you are satisfied with it, make several photocopies. You will use them when you purchase materials and supplies, and again during construction.

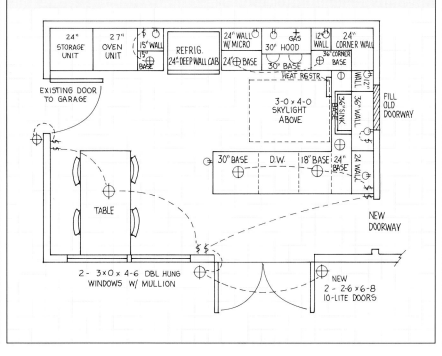

Choosing Countertops

The countertops are a dominant design element in any kitchen. You can use the same material for all the countertops to create a uniform appearance, or you can use different materials to meet different functional needs. Use waterproof materials near the sink, heat-resistant materials next to the cooktop and oven, butcher block for a cutting surface, marble or other stone for rolling out dough, and extradurable materials in a kitchen subject to enthusiastic use.

No matter what material you choose for the counters, you will have to make decisions about the edge and corner details. You will also have to decide how high the back splash should be and what material it should be made of.

Laminates

A thin laminate veneer glued to a backing of plywood or particleboard has long been a favorite countertop material. It comes in a wide choice of colors and patterns, can be heat formed to create a continuous back splash, is easy to maintain, and is relatively inexpensive. It is subject to scratches and scorching and it shows seams. The exposed edges of the older types of laminate reveal the core as a dark line, which destroys the look of a flawless, uniform surface; but the newer, solid-core laminates do not present this problem. The seams are invisible and there is no distracting dark line around the edges. The newer laminates can also be inlaid with contrasting material to dress up the edges of the countertop.

Ceramic Tile

Ceramic tile is durable, heat resistant, and colorful. It is not inherently waterproof, because of the grout lines, but it can be made so with proper installation. It lends itself well to odd-shaped spaces. In style it ranges from traditional to contemporary, from casual to formal, depending on the color, the pattern, and the grout. It imposes a strong grid pattern on the counter if the grout is a color that contrasts with the tiles. Tile allows you to express yourself with creative layouts and decorative accents. You can even design your own tiles and have them made to order. Tile comes in unlimited colors and patterns, but these tend to follow the current fads. The surface can be uneven—and unforgiving if you drop glassware on it. Edges can be trimmed with special edge caps or wood strips. Tile makes an excellent back splash, which is sometimes carried all the way to the ceiling.

Butcher Block

Wood has a warm, natural appearance that softens the smooth surfaces and hard edges of a kitchen. Butcher block comes in various lengths and a standard 25-inch width, but two widths can be laminated together to form a wide countertop. It makes an excellent cutting surface, but it needs to be maintained to prevent it from drying out. Soil buildup can also be a problem, but stains can be sanded. Butcher block should not be installed near sinks because the wood will warp if it stays wet.

Solid Surface Materials

Originally a substitute for marble, these composite materials come in solid colors and in patterns resembling granite and marble. They are known by the brand names Corian, Avonite, and 2000X, among others. They are lightweight and can be cut and worked into any shape. Seams are concealed, producing a flawless expanse of smooth material. Light scratches, most stains, and scorches can be sanded out, but the material should not be used as a cutting surface. Edges can be decorated with various trims and inlays or built up to give the appearance of a thicker slab.

Slab and Dimensioned Stone

Marble, granite, and slate are available in full slabs and in tiles, which are called dimensioned stone. Although they are more expensive than many of the alternatives, these countertops are beautiful and durable. Natural stone adds a timeless elegance to traditional kitchen styles and a rich, polished look to contemporary styles. Colors vary. Stone resists heat and hard wear very well, but marble can stain and is vulnerable to acids. It is best used in a baking center, as a confectioner's slab for rolling out pastry.

Slab stone countertops are usually sold cut to fit, although standard sizes are often available. Shop around while you are working out the floor plan. Using a standard-sized countertop could be good financially.

Dimensioned-stone tiles are usually sold in 12-inch squares. They are installed using the same techniques used to set ceramic tile (see page 92).

Choosing Lighting

Plan the lighting as you develop the floor plans. For daytime use, bring in as much natural light as possible. If the illumination comes from only one window, it will create glare and contrasts of light and shadow. Try to plan windows on at least two different walls, or use a skylight to balance the illumination from a single window. French doors, a greenhouse window, and high windows above the cabinets will also serve to increase the natural light. Some windows will receive intense sunlight during certain times of the day or during certain seasons. Morning sun and winter sun are usually welcome, but you may need to provide shades to soften both. A west-facing window subject to hot afternoon sun and a clear skylight should be shaded from the outside.

Plan artificial lighting to provide both general illumination and task lighting. There are several ways to accomplish both goals. One is to install recessed lights over all the counters and work areas. They focus light where it is needed for specific tasks, but throw off enough ambient light to provide general illumination as well. However, the load should be divided among two or three switch loops so that someone walking through the kitchen at night won't have to turn on all the lights. Use dimmers and multiple switching to solve the problem.

Another approach is to use an overhead fixture, such as a pendant or surface globe, for general illumination. Then arrange task lighting on separate switches wherever it is needed, using recessed fixtures, track lights, or undercabinet fluorescent tubes.

A third approach is to install a luminous ceiling over the entire kitchen, using fluorescent tubes. This eliminates shadows and creates an even light all around, but since the tubes must be all on or all off, it too creates an either/or situation.

You can also plan accent lighting to provide special effects. Highlight a display of glassware with a spotlight or cabinet lighting to create a stunning effect at night, or conceal strip lights above picture moldings, around window frames, or beneath toe kicks to create dramatic moods.

Consider the color as well as the intensity of light. Fluorescent lighting ranges from warm colors, which flatter skin tones and make food look appetizing, to cool colors, which accentuate a blue or green decor, to daylight bulbs, which have a cooling effect in hot climates. Incandescent bulbs give off a warm light.

Lighting affects your safety, health, energy, and efficiency. It is also an important element in design. Therefore, you may want to seek professional advice in planning the lighting scheme. A few hours of consultation with an interior designer or lighting specialist will go a long way toward creating a cheery, dramatic kitchen.

Choosing Appliances

In selecting appliances, consider size, color, performance, design features, and energy conservation. Use the brochures and other information that you collected, along with your survey to help you to select products. The following sections offer some general design guidelines for choosing appliances.

Cooktops and Ranges

A cooktop is a surface cooking unit, with no oven, which is inserted into a countertop. A freestanding range includes a surface cooking unit and one or more ovens and is intended to stand alone. A slide-in range is similar to a freestanding range but is designed with raised edges so that it

Adding a bay window brought more light into this room and opened up the view to the adjoining deck and yard, making doing dishes almost fun. The sleek double sink was cast in one piece with the solid surface–material countertop.

can fit between two cabinets. A drop-in range has surface cooking units and an oven; it is built into a cabinet and countertop.

A cooktop built into the counter can be placed almost anywhere, frees up valuable cabinet space for storage, and does not interrupt the continuous line created by the edge of the countertop. Many models come with grills, griddles, deep fryers, and other specialized accessories. These can be added to the basic burner unit to create a versatile, integrated cooking center, or installed somewhere else where they will be out of the way and perhaps closer to the point of use. A range, however, is more efficient in terms of utility hookups and compact space.

The traditional differences between gas and electric cooking are becoming blurred as improvements are made in both types of appliances. The choice may come down to a question of which form of energy is more economical in your area. Today's gas appliances have pilotless ignition, which saves fuel and reduces heat buildup, and they come with the option of a thermostatically controlled burner, which maintains a constant temperature throughout the cooking cycle. Some gas cooktops come with stainless steel or white grates that blend in with modern color schemes. The most dramatic improvements, however, have been made in electric appliances. Burners heat up almost instantly, infinite-heat controls can be set at any level, and again you have the option of a thermostatically controlled burner. The appearance of these appliances has also changed. Traditional coil elements are still available, but continuous glass tops with heating elements below them and individual burners that look like discs provide a sleeker look. One type of electric cooktop does not even get hot. By means of magnetic induction it induces a steel or iron pot to heat up on its own. The look is as revolutionary as the method—multiple-"burner" units have a smooth, uninterrupted

surface; individual units look like ceramic tiles set into the countertop. Only cookware made of iron, steel, or steel alloys works with this system.

Commercial ranges offer some advantages. They have large ovens, high heat, and generous-sized burners, but plan carefully before you decide to buy one. They require a heavy-duty ventilating system and the code requires that you maintain a clearance between the unit and all surrounding surfaces—which must be noncombustible. Commercial ranges burn hot, requiring heavy-duty cookware, and can generate enough heat to make the kitchen very uncomfortable. The range can also look cumbersome and institutional. One way to solve some of these problems is to opt for the burner unit only and use it with a standard residential oven. Another solution is to buy a commercial-style range designed for home use, an option that several manufacturers now offer. These units are more compact and generate less heat than a commercial range; they can be installed with zero clearance; and they have pilotless ignition. Most units come with a standard black or stainless steel finish, but at least one line includes a cooktop unit in colors.

Another factor to consider in choosing a cooktop or a range is the arrangement of the burners. Consider too the location of the controls and whether you plan to install the unit in a place where it will require a down-draft ventilating system.

Vents/Hoods

Mechanical ventilation—either a range hood or a down-draft system—eliminates cooking odors, excess water vapor, and the buildup of potential contaminants. For a hood mounted against a wall, the venting system should be rated to move air at 450 to 650 CFM (cubic feet per minute). For a hood mounted above a peninsula or an island, the required ratings are 650 to 900 CFM and 900 to 1000 CFM respectively. Also consider noise. Look for a sound rating of

8 sones or less. Some ventilating systems have the fan unit mounted on the roof or on an exterior wall instead of inside the hood.

A range hood should extend slightly beyond the cooktop burners. Because the hood is near eye level, it is noticeable; pay attention to its appearance. There are many styles to choose from: low hoods mounted under a wall cabinet, full-height units, concealed units that swing out for use, and suspended island hoods. Most of these units come in a choice of finishes. If you like, conceal them behind cabinets.

Choosing appliances may mean retaining your current ones. This beautiful stove worked perfectly and fit well into the classic kitchen theme that the homeowners had chosen. The stove was looking a bit worn, however, so the owners sent it out to an auto-body shop for repainting and rechroming while their kitchen was under construction.

Ovens

Ovens can look awkward and they can be difficult to reach, so plan the the new unit carefully. If you don't mind bending slightly to use an oven, consider an undercounter model. Some of these are installed below a cooktop unit, but if you bake a lot you will have to put up with the heat while you use the cooktop. Wall ovens are more convenient to reach and easier to see into. Choose a model with clean lines and a style that will blend into the cabinetry. If you have white cabinets, choose an oven with a white front for a unified look. Black glass provides a striking accent that can be incorporated into many kitchen styles.

Beside appearance, consider both interior and exterior size. You may have to balance desired capacity against available space, so shop carefully to find the most efficient model. Installing an oven next to a refrigerator will not usually create a problem because both appliances are well insulated. However, check to see whether either manufacturer recommends that you maintain a clearance, just in case.

Consider your style of cooking. You may want two ovens in different locations. You will also have to decide whether to get a conventional oven, a convection oven, a combination conventional-convection oven, a microwave-convection oven, or a double unit with a conventional oven below and a microwave-convection oven above. Choose according to your preference, but also consider energy use. Consult with a kitchen specialist or with an appliance dealer whose staff includes kitchen designers in order to make sure that you have considered all the advantages and disadvantages of each type.

Microwave Ovens

You probably worked out the location of a separate microwave oven in your preliminary design. The only details left to consider are doorswing, style, and size.

Refrigerator–Freezers

Planning a refrigerator involves more than deciding where to put the Big Box. Also consider storage requirements, door arrangements, external size, and visual impact. Your food-buying habits and cooking style and the shortcomings of your present refrigerator will help you to decide what you want in the new unit.

If you want a combination refrigerator-freezer, as most families do, you have three choices. Side-by-side units have narrow doors, an advantage where space is tight, but the doorswings cannot be reversed. They also use more energy than the other units and very large items will not fit in the freezer. If you choose a freezer-over model, you may find it hard to get into the refrigerator but very easy to get into the freezer. In the freezer-under model, the refrigerator is at the ideal height.

Most refrigerators extend out from the cabinetry, but several manufacturers offer built-in models that fit flush with a standard 24-inch cabinet. In most cases the doors are covered with panels that match the adjacent cabinets. The exposed ventilating grill and ice maker are the only visible evidence of an appliance. In some units, however, the appliance is completely concealed behind conventional cabinet doors. As you open the cabinet door, the appliance door swings open with it.

For tight spaces or separate bar areas, consider either a compact refrigerator-freezer designed for apartment use or two separate undercounter units.

Dishwashers

All built-in dishwashers are 24 inches wide, except for an occasional 18-inch model, and all of them fit either under the countertop or under the sink. The main options involve performance and the color and style of the front. Most manufacturers provide changeable front panels in stock colors or custom panels to match the cabinets.

Choosing Sinks and Faucets

Sinks come in a variety of sizes, colors, materials, bowl configurations, and rim details. For food preparation, a single bowl is usually adequate. A sink that handles both cleanup and food preparation should have a double bowl. For corner installations, use an L-shaped sink or install an angled cabinet and use a conventional sink. Consider too the depth of the bowl. If you fill and clean large pots, make sure that one of the bowls is extra deep and plan a faucet with a gooseneck spout or sprayer. Shape is another consideration. Most sinks are rectangular, but round sinks are available in single-bowl or double-bowl configurations.

Sink manufacturers provide a considerable choice of materials and colors. Stainless steel comes in polished or matte finishes. Enameled cast iron comes in a wide range of colors, as well as in white and black. Sinks made of lightweight composite materials, such as compressed quartz, come in white or in colors.

Another important design element to consider when choosing a sink is how the unit is mounted and how the mounting affects the rim detail. One option is to mount the sink beneath the surface of the counter so that no rim shows. Instead, the countertop material covers the edge of the sink. This method can be used only with countertops of tile, stone, or solid surface materials. Another option is to mount the sink on top of the counter so that its own rim shows, making a sharp delineation between the sink and the countertop material. A third method is to install the sink with a separate metal rim, which also emphasizes the outline of the sink.

Faucets also come in a bewildering array of styles—and prices. Remember that the faucet is a focal point of the kitchen, so consider the overall kitchen style when you choose the style and color of the faucet.

Drawing Elevations

A floor plan is adequate for planning general layout, but you need elevation drawings to fine-tune the design, and particularly to evaluate storage potential. Using the preliminary plan as a reference, draw an elevation plan of each wall. Use the same techniques as you used to draw the base plan. Do separate elevations for each island and peninsula.

First draw the outline of the wall and block in permanent features, such as windows and doorways. Next, draw the countertops and appliances. You will also have made some basic decisions concerning the cabinetry, such as the locations of the tall storage units, the sink unit, and the corner cabinets. To plan the rest of the cabinets, make tracings of the elevation you have done so far and doodle in possible cabinet schemes to fill it out. First think through the activities that take place in each work center and decide where things should be stored for convenient access. Would it be easier to find a certain item in a drawer, an upper cabinet, or a lower cabinet? Would you be reaching for it

with your right hand or your left hand? Can a large, bulky item be stored elsewhere to make more room? As ideas emerge, jot them down on the plan and draw a quick circle around them—you do not have to sketch in actual cabinets yet. Add items to each circle as you think of them, until you have worked out ways of meeting all of your storage needs.

Now make a new tracing, and plan the actual cabinets. For exact widths and heights, consult one of your cabinet brochures. Be as detailed as you can when you sketch in the cabinets. Indicate the doorswings, the exact height of the drawers, and the positions of the shelves. You may have to adjust the floor plan as you go.

Follow the same procedure for each wall elevation. Take your time. An extra few hours of finessing at this point could make the difference between storage units that are exactly what you want and storage units that aren't quite right. Considering what a big slice of the budgetary pie cabinets represent, it's time well spent.

Faucets have a sculptural quality, which you should also consider. Before you get lost in faucet fantasyland, make sure you are comfortable operating the unit. Grip the handle, adjust the temperature, swing the spout, and operate the sprayer—all under kitchen battle conditions.

Choosing Flooring

A kitchen floor must be durable, easy to clean, and comfortable to stand on. It must also be beautiful enough to fulfill its role as a major design element. Next to material, color is the most important factor in choosing a kitchen floor. Solid color floors create a calm, serene effect, but they may show scratches and dirt easily. Some resilient floorings and ceramic tiles come in textured patterns that minimize these problems. A finely patterned floor in neutral tones works well in most kitchens because it does not overshadow the other elements of the design. The color of such a floor should be just a shade darker than the walls and ceiling. A bold pattern may conflict with other focal points, and it could dominate a small space.

Resilient flooring is a popular choice. It is relatively inexpensive, easy to clean, and comfortable to walk on. The variety of patterns and colors is almost unlimited.

Ceramic tile is beautiful and durable but not at all resilient. Consider the size and color of the grout lines as carefully as you consider the tile itself. Contrasting grout creates a bold grid pattern that may overwhelm the room. White tile creates a bright and sunny effect, but it shows dirt. Dimensioned-stone tiles, brick veneers, and similar materials create a beautiful, substantial look, but the hard surface has no resilience and it reflects sound.

Hardwood flooring is a good choice for kitchens because it is somewhat resilient and yet fairly durable if it is installed and finished properly. Natural colors impart a rich, warm feeling. Pickling or bleaching gives it a snappy, fresh look.

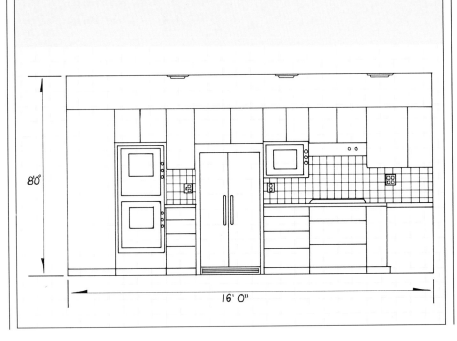

Choosing Wall Finishes

With cabinets, back splashes, appliances, pass-throughs, and doorways taking up most of the kitchen, there may not be much wall space left. Using the same wall treatments throughout the kitchen and the surrounding rooms is a fine way to merge these areas into a kitchen suite. On the other hand, if the kitchen is large, using a variety of wall finishes adds interest and defines important architectural features.

Wallcoverings with small, subtle patterns are very effective, adding texture, color, richness, and warmth.

Custom tile, textured plaster, exotic hardwoods, stainless steel, lacquer, laminates, and special paint effects are all used to cover kitchen walls. However, such materials must be used with caution. If the cabinets, counters, and fixtures are richly colored or patterned, or if they vary in shape, size, line, and color, busy wall coverings will tend to conflict with, or neutralize, their visual effect.

Choosing Ceiling Finishes

As you concentrate on the floor plan and elevations it is very easy to overlook the ceiling. However, the ceiling is as important as any other element in the kitchen design.

Any variation from a standard 8-foot flat ceiling adds interest and drama. A high ceiling makes a room look formal and also creates an illusion of greater space. A ceiling with multiple heights creates movement and animation. A skylight or other interruption serves as a focal point.

Beams and soffits can be used to alter the apparent shape of a room. An open soffit pulls the eye upward, making the room look higher. Beams and soffits running across the narrow dimension of a long room make it feel more square.

Alternative ceiling treatments can be used to break up a large room into distinct areas, setting apart the eating area from the food preparation center, for example.

The color of a ceiling also affects spatial perception. A light ceiling feels farther away; a dark ceiling feels closer. A ceiling covered with siding, paneling, or any similar board treatment draws the eye upward.

Choosing Finishing Details

Cabinet hardware, trim, racks, light fixtures, personal objects on display, plants, and art may seem like afterthoughts, but they are important design elements too. They can tie the kitchen together and give it a sense of style, or they can sabotage the whole design. If the rest of the house has a distinct style and the style of the kitchen is different, you may be able to use hardware, trim, or other details to provide continuity. Plan every detail, from the soap dispenser to the paper-towel holder, with the overall design of the kitchen in mind.

Do not ignore the kick space below base cabinets. Instead, turn it into an asset. One of these shallow drawers contains canned goods; the other is fitted for a stepladder. Other drawers in the kick space around this room are used to store recyclables, bulk paper products, and sodas purchased by the case.

The guidelines presented in the first chapter can only begin to convey the myriad decisions that each homeowner must make in the course of designing a new kitchen. Experience is the best teacher. This chapter presents profiles of six real kitchens, all of which have recently been remodeled. These are all kitchens where real people cook, and those people faced the same kind of problems and constraints that you may be facing now. They found solutions, which they have been kind enough to share. The families include a busy, two-income couple with a passion for entertaining, a family with several small children, empty nesters who waited 15 years to remodel their kitchen, and a single woman who wanted to make the most of a very small space. The houses range from a 1920s cottage that badly needed updating to a 1950s custom home to tract homes that lacked a personal touch. Read on to see how these homeowners have solved common problems; made compromises; and chosen styles, colors, textures, and materials. Understanding how they did it—and seeing the beautiful photographic results—will give you the confidence to make your own decisions.

The needs of a growing family dictated many of the decisions concerning the design of this large, modern-style kitchen. Located in the middle of the house, with access to the backyard, family room, and dining room, it truly is the center of the home.

SPACE FOR A LARGE FAMILY

This modern kitchen with a country feel is focused on family life. The owners have four young children, and they wanted a light, open kitchen that would serve as the hub of indoor and outdoor activities for the whole family. The kitchen is nestled into the rear of the house and faces the spacious backyard.

This large kitchen has three doors leading to other parts of the house and two doors leading outside. Usually only one person does the cooking, so there was no need to design special features to accommodate several cooks, but there is plenty of room for aspiring young chefs to help prepare meals in the future. An extensive baking center wasn't needed either, since this family doesn't do much baking. The more immediate need was for lots of eating space.

A large island separates the main work area from the traffic lanes. The edges of the island align with the various walls and corners of the kitchen, mirroring the angles in the basic house design. Part of the island serves as an eating counter. A large ceiling fixture is aligned with the longest side of the island, giving it further definition and harmonizing with the overall lines of the kitchen.

The refrigerator is separated from the work island by a traffic lane, but it is convenient to the family room and the patio, and it can be reached without entering the main work area near the sink and cooktop. There is no counter space next to the refrigerator, but the island and cooktop counters are only a step or two away. The gas cooktop includes an electric barbecue grill and a down-draft vent. The sink faucet has a detachable sprayer built into the spout.

The oven center, which is outside of the main work area, includes two single ovens and a built-in microwave. There is ample counter space directly beneath the microwave and

Opposite: Three ovens and a large side-by-side refrigerator make it easy to cook for a crowd. Plan counter space near ovens and refrigerators for measuring out ingredients and setting down hot dishes.
Bottom: *Accessories, light fixtures, and furnishings contribute to a kitchen's theme. An old-style pendant lamp and tie-on chair cushions give this eating area its country charm.*

on the nearby island. A desk alcove next to the refrigerator serves as a communication and planning center.

The countertops are 3-inch by 3-inch white ceramic tile with white grout. The edges are trimmed with oak strips stained to match the floor, giving the kitchen a strong horizontal line. The sink is recessed and rimmed with bullnose tiles. The overhang for the island eating area has extra braces to keep the tile countertop from cracking under pressure.

The kitchen lends itself well to entertaining. There is convenient access to the dining room, entry, and outdoors. Guests can circulate around the work area while remaining outside

it. The island and the long peninsula counter make it easy to serve a light snack or a complete buffet.

The windows and glass doors that enclose the eating area offer sweeping views of the backyard from every point in the kitchen. They admit natural light and can be left open on warm days to create an indoor-outdoor eating area. The curve of the window wall adds dynamic interest to the kitchen space and balances the angles in the work area.

The wall at the opposite end of the kitchen was just wide enough to accommodate three storage units. One of these units includes a cooler for bottled water. Open shelves in the center unit help to break up the

space and offer an attractive area for displaying personal objects. Pantry shelves line the third unit.

Recessed fixtures over the traffic lanes provide general illumination. The luminous panel fixture over the island and fluorescent tubes under the wall cabinets provide task lighting for the work areas, and the special fixture over the table adds an interesting design accent.

The overall style of this kitchen is contemporary with a country theme. The white laminate cabinets, white tile, plain white ceiling, and wood counter edging emphasize the clean, fresh lines. The random-width oak flooring, the antique cabinet over the sink, and the heirloom dining set lend a touch of rustic informality. The wallcovering, a delicate floral pattern on a white background, accentuates the country theme. Finishing touches are the charming light fixture over the table, the traditional moldings, and a few well-chosen antiques on display.

Top: *Some manufacturers provide complete lines of products for use in kitchen decoration. Matching fabric is used for window treatments and wallcovering to tie this room together. Matching decorated tiles, kitchenware, canisters, and other accents are often available as well. Along with the fine print of the window and wall fabric, selected antiques, such as an old pharmacy cabinet, and handcrafted accessories create an American country theme in this modern kitchen.*
Opposite: *Consider all your storage needs when planning your kitchen cabinet systems. Include a place for a fire extinguisher and an emergency first-aid kit and make sure every family member knows where both are located as well as how to use them.*

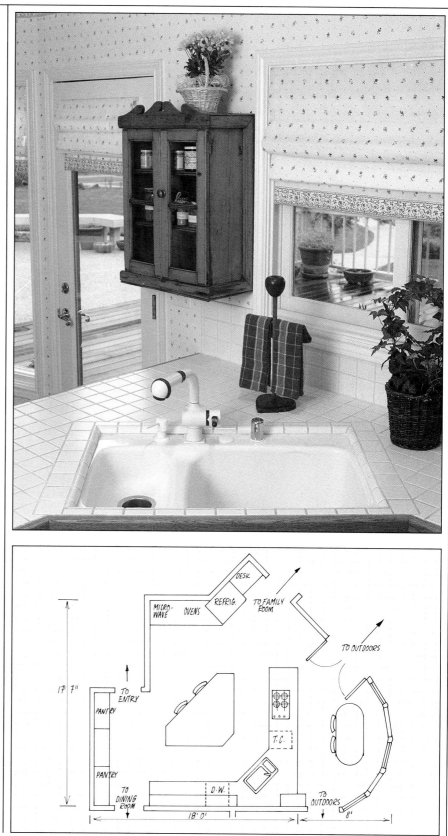

SIMPLE PERFECTION

The original kitchen for this simple home was a hodge-podge of conflicting space, horrendous colors, and outdated improvements. The owner's goals were to make the limited space more efficient, to update the appliances, and to have the style of the kitchen be in keeping with the rest of the house, a 1920s cottage on a wooded hillside.

Originally, the stove was a large range that occupied most of one side of the kitchen without benefit of either counters or storage shelves. The refrigerator was equally large, and the door could not be opened fully without banging into the stove. An unattractive built-in light fixture that partially blocked the windows and a mismatched patchwork of assorted appliances, countertop materials, and floor covering added to the overall confusion. Large cabinet pulls kept bruising the owner's knees.

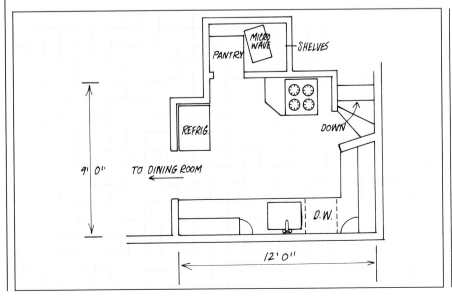

Top: *Repeating the grid pattern, from the tile back splash to the vinyl sheet flooring to the cooktop surround, gives this kitchen a cohesive design.*
Opposite: *Installing a new laminate countertop on an existing bank of base cabinets refreshed the whole look of this cozy kitchen. Remodeling needn't be extensive to be effective.*

The main goals of remodeling were to solve the space conflicts, create a more efficient work area, and unify the kitchen into a simple and harmonious whole. This was accomplished by retaining some of the original features, such as the windows and some cabinets, and replacing the rest. There was no room to expand the basic floor plan, so the first task was to make the most of the limited space. A skylight was added, which visually expanded the space, and the old false ceiling was removed. The

new ceiling is coved to match the ceiling in the adjacent dining room. The greatest transformation was achieved by replacing the old stove with a carefully designed cooking center. The compact gas cooktop and undercounter electric oven match the scale of the small kitchen. The angled edges of the countertop provide just enough clearance around the tight corners on each side. A cumbersome cupboard above the old stove was replaced with a more streamlined unit that includes a retractable vent/hood, creating more open space at eye level.

There was just enough space next to the doorway for a 24-inch-deep built-in refrigerator. The recessed design creates an uncluttered profile and facilitates access to the pantry. The original kitchen included the rather large pantry, but it was not used as fully as it might have been because of the restricted access. Replacing the old refrigerator with a built-in model and removing the door to the pantry created easy access and visibility. There is even a large shelf in the pantry for a microwave oven and other appliances that took up valuable counter space.

The original plywood cabinets were in good condition and only needed repainting. They were upgraded by fitting them with pull-out trays and storage organizers. The knobs on the old cabinets were replaced with stylish metal pulls that fold down flat when not in use. One of the lower cabinets had been a California cooler—an enclosed cupboard with screened vents to the outside. In many older homes in mild climates these coolers were used to keep fruits and vegetables fresh. With the help of some pull-out trays and modern wire baskets, this cabinet is once again being used for its original purpose—to store bulk food items and produce.

The green-and-white color scheme, which gives the kitchen a fresh, crisp look, is carried throughout the tile work, the laminate countertop, and the vinyl floor covering. The potentially monotonous grid pattern of the tiles is broken up by a band of diagonal grout lines and by reversing the tile and grout colors on opposite sides of the room.

The thoughtful planning and careful attention to detail in this simple, small kitchen show how a partial remodeling can transform a functional disaster and visual eyesore into an elegant and timeless masterpiece.

ADDING OLD-WORLD CHARM

This charming and efficient kitchen occupies a space that was originally divided into a laundry, kitchen, and hall. Access from the kitchen to the rest of the house, including the dining room, was through the hallway. There was only one window, and the kitchen felt very dark and cavelike, even though the window offered a spectacular view. The owners enjoy entertaining—they especially like giving dinner parties—but the tight space in the kitchen and the indirect access to the other rooms made it difficult, if not impossible, for whoever was in the kitchen to interact.

The first design goal was to create a greater sense of openness within the kitchen, and between the kitchen and the dining room, while keeping the two rooms distinct and staying within the awkward shape imposed by the angles of the house. Part of the solution was to remove the walls between the kitchen, laundry, and hallway to create a larger space for the new kitchen. A 7-foot-long bay window, 5-foot-wide French doors, and a 3- by 4-foot skylight opened the space to the outdoors and made it feel larger. Access to the dining room

Top: *Exposing the back of a chimney added the charm of brick to the French country theme of this room and provided enough space to install a small bar. Note the careful cutting to fit the cabinet against the brick. It was done by first drawing a cardboard pattern and then tracing it onto the wood.*
Opposite: *Interesting patterns of sunshine from the skylight play across this kitchen throughout the day. The automated skylight also vents excess heat and odors, captures breezes, and closes automatically if it starts to rain.*

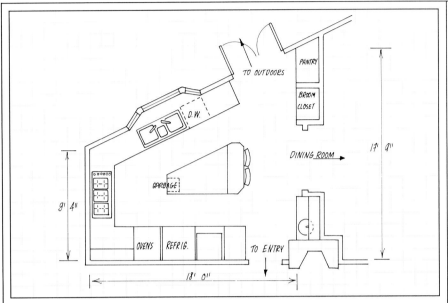

was improved by creating a new double doorway to replace the original single door that was located in an alcove now occupied by a bar sink. A pair of stained-glass doors now separates the kitchen from the dining room. When these doors are left open, the kitchen feels larger and the dining room is enhanced with natural light from the kitchen. When they are shut at night, light from the kitchen illuminates the stained glass for dramatic dining effects.

The compact and efficient floor plan concentrates all the traffic lanes at one end of the kitchen. The rest of the space is a work triangle with an island. A large, commercial-style cooktop anchors the farthest corner, and the sink and refrigerator occupy opposite sides of the island. The double ovens are within the work triangle. The upper unit is a combination microwave-convection oven; the lower unit is a conventional oven.

The aisles on two sides of the island are only 32 inches wide, but the generous floor area at the far end

(roughly 5 feet square), the tapered island, and the bay window behind the sink combine to create a spacious feeling.

Several features make it possible for two or more cooks to work in this kitchen at the same time. The bar sink with its small counter area is convenient to the main island. There are three pull-out cutting boards—one at the narrow end of the island, one to the right of the dishwasher, and one in the island opposite the washer-dryer closet—each of which serves as a separate work station. The raised eating counter provides a comfortable place for guests to gather without being in the cook's way. The stained-glass double doors leading to the dining room eliminate a potential bottleneck.

The owners wanted a kitchen style that combines modern efficiency with old-world charm to match the European country style used throughout the rest of the house. A collection of copper-ware pieces, which they wanted to display in the kitchen, set the tone for many of the aesthetic decisions. The blue of the cabinet stain complements the color of the

copper and creates a traditional, almost antique, feeling. The floor is African slate, which is a coppery brown rather than the more usual gray or green. The stained glass is in the same color range. The countertops are white solid surface material and the wood inlay around the edges is stained to match the cabinets. All of the countertops are a standard 36 inches high, except the eating counter, which is 43 inches high.

The narrow end of the kitchen constituted a natural focal point that required more than a blank wall or a run of cabinets. The answer was a copper range hood over the cooktop and a custom tile mural depicting an array of meats. The border tiles around the mural are the same color as the cabinet stain.

The brick chimney and fireplace were a pleasant surprise, discovered when the walls were opened up. They were part of the original house—the kitchen area had been added on—and the aging brickwork suited the new kitchen very well.

Because the old laundry was removed to create more space for the new kitchen, the owners had to decide where to relocate the washer and dryer. There was room in the basement, but they decided to make space in the kitchen for an over-under unit; they wanted the laundry convenient to the rest of the house and easy to use while they were in the kitchen. It was a successful decision—the owners now spend a great deal of time in their new kitchen and even use the island as a handy table for folding laundry.

Opposite: The original layout took no advantage of the spectacular view beyond the kitchen walls. Now the great oak in the backyard can be appreciated in all its glory.

A COOK'S DELIGHT

Above all, this is a working kitchen. The owners are avid cooks who enjoy sharing their culinary enthusiasm with family and friends. Not only do they cook as often as possible, but they prepare sauces, make pasta, and can foods in large quantities as well.

Because they had such specific needs and because they valued organization and convenience, these homeowners spent over two years planning the kitchen—after living in the house for over 15 years. Then they engaged a professional to put together the final design. As a result, there is a space for everything and it is all easy to reach.

The centerpiece of this kitchen is an island over 4 feet wide and 13 feet long. The island has a sink on each side and a 7-inch-thick butcher block at one end. Each sink has its own dishwasher, towel rack, and garbage bin. The island divides the kitchen into two work areas, one for cooking and the other for baking. To minimize trips between these two areas, duplicate sets of cooking equipment are stored on both sides in the drawers and cabinets.

Opposite: *These homeowners are avid bakers, so a complete baking center was a definite priority in their kitchen design plan. This low counter makes rolling dough easy on a cook's back; the dowels at the end of the counter pull out to form a pasta-drying rack.*

Bottom: *It took several workers to hoist the 7-inch-thick butcher block into place on the center island. That's a garbage drawer in the center of the island. The tambour door at the right is an appliance garage.*

Charming handcrafted tiles depict favorite cooking ingredients: rabbit, fish, sausage, mushrooms, peppers, garlic, and herbs. Because canning is a popular activity in this house, a special water fixture was plumbed high enough to fill large pots.

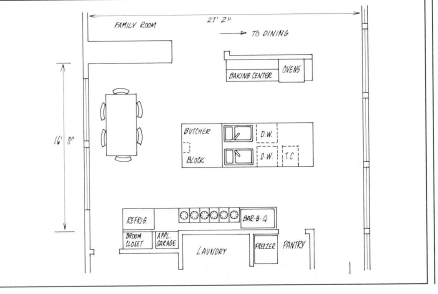

FAMILY ROOM

27' 2"

→ TO DINING

BAKING CENTER | OVENS

16' 0"

BUTCHER | D.W.
BLOCK | D.W. | T.C.

REFRIG. | BAR-B-Q

BROOM CLOSET | APPL. GARAGE | LAUNDRY | FREEZER | PANTRY

The cooking area has six single-burner commercial cooktops and a barbecue grill, all arrayed in a single line to allow several cooks to work at once. A water spigot over one of the burners makes it possible to fill large pots on the spot, so that the cook doesn't have to lug them from the sink. There is a 9-foot stainless steel vent/hood over the cooking area, and the countertop and back splash are covered with 6-inch tiles. The decorative tiles for the back splash were custom made; they depict some of the ingredients that these cooks enjoy using in their dishes. The appliance garage and wall cabinet at the end of the cooking area are recessed into the wall to maintain a clean, uncluttered look and keep the countertop as open as possible. A tambour door hides the appliances.

The baking center has a lower countertop than the island (it is 33 inches high instead of the standard 36 inches), making it easier to roll out dough. The surface, like that of the island, is polished granite. The base cabinets are all drawer units rather than shelves. Some of the deep drawers contain bins for flour and other baking supplies. Spices are stored in a shallow drawer; like the cooking utensils, they are duplicated in an identical drawer beside the cooktop. Decorative jars of foods are displayed on the shelves at the end of the baking center, below the built-in pasta-drying rack.

A walk-in pantry with a see-through door and a tile floor provides storage for bulk items, home-canned foods, and wine. It includes a stand-up freezer and also provides access to the adjacent laundry room.

One of the design problems, as with any large kitchen, was to keep everything in human scale, so that the space would not appear over-whelming. This was achieved by

changing the ceiling levels at the midpoint, by using warm earth tones for the color scheme, and by bringing the wall cabinets up to the lower ceiling and maintaining this line throughout the kitchen. The large window areas at both ends of the kitchen also help to keep it in scale by emphasizing the wider panorama outdoors. Oversized materials and furnishings likewise serve to maintain a sense of proportion. The thick edges of the counters, the massive butcher-block table with its high-backed chairs, the large sinks, the double-wide refrigerator, and the massive exposed beams all are scaled to the size of the room.

The cabinets are rift-sawn oak. Their tight, parallel grain pattern enhances the monochromatic color scheme. Together with the oak strip flooring, the bronze-colored granite, and the off-white tiles, they create the feeling of refined elegance that characterizes this informal but uncluttered kitchen.

A common problem—what to do with the garbage disposer switch on a center island—was cleverly solved in this kitchen. The switch is covered by the drawer that holds the pull-out towel rack.

LETTING THE SUN SHINE IN

T*he main problem in remodeling this kitchen was converting a warren of small rooms, closets, alcoves, pantries, and hallways into a simplified, harmonious space. The original kitchen was small and dark, with few windows. It could not be used during the day without turning on the lights. The owners wanted the new kitchen to be open, spacious, and full of natural light.*

The transformation was accomplished by removing all of the partition walls, adding windows and skylights, relocating the dining-room door, removing a chimney, and incorporating a basement stairway into the central storage closet. What emerged is an expansive, airy kitchen with an efficient work space, a large eating and activity area, and plenty of storage in the adjacent closet and laundry.

The basic plan revolves around a work triangle formed by the refrigerator, sink, and cooktop. The cooktop consists of four commercial burners laid out in a straight line, to allow two or three cooks to use it at once. To conserve energy and reduce heat buildup, only one pilot light is left permanently on. The sink and clean-up center are conveniently close to both the informal eating area and the

Opposite: *Space for a large refrigerator and a good-sized storage unit was found underneath the stairway. This clever solution freed up enough square footage for a breakfast room.*

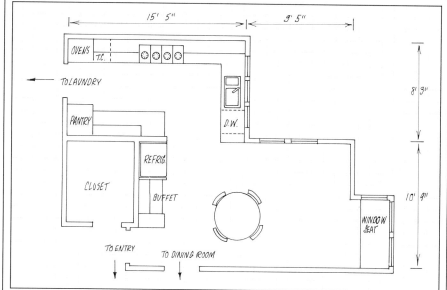

dining room. The sink has extra deep bowls for large pots and pans. The refrigerator is a built-in model with the freezer unit on the bottom. There is counter space on both sides.

A microwave oven and a compact double oven, all built into a conventional oven cabinet, are outside the basic work triangle but convenient to the main counter. A trash compactor is tucked under the counter next to the ovens.

The long counters provide at least four separate work stations, making it possible for several people to cook at once: In this family, the children often help to prepare the meals. The counter next to the refrigerator doubles as additional eating space. It has a 4-inch back splash of the solid surface material in contrast to the tile back splash on the opposite counter.

Natural light floods the work area through tall windows over the sink and two skylights in the ceiling. The breakfast room receives light through two tall new windows and through the original windows above the cozy window seat. The main windows face east, so the kitchen receives direct morning sun. Overheating through the skylights isn't a problem because

trees and adjacent buildings block the sun during the hottest seasons.

The color scheme of pastel earth tones, including the light green tile, beige painted walls, and strip oak flooring, reflects the outdoor palette of natural colors. It also blends remarkably well with a favorite painting the owners chose to hang in the breakfast area. The white laminate cabinets and white solid-composite countertops set off the colors and give the kitchen a fresh, clean look.

The cabinets and shelves include many specialized storage features, such as a narrow cabinet for place mats next to the dishwasher. Most of the base cabinets have drawers and pullouts instead of fixed shelves.

During the initial stages of remodeling, a chimney was discovered in the corner near the window seat. At first the owners were going to leave it, and clean up the exposed bricks or possibly paint them to match the color scheme. However, the bulky mass tended to throw the room out of balance and disrupt its clean lines. The owners considered several ways of incorporating the two-story chimney into the overall design, but they finally decided to remove it and the fireplace outright. This drastic step was the catalyst that brought the entire project together and created the light, open kitchen of their dreams.

Opposite: An enormous amount of storage space is obtained by installing a rack system in a full-height pantry cupboard.
Top: The back splashes in this kitchen extend all the way to the bottom of the wall cabinets. This makes cleanup easier and eliminates the need to paint the area.
Bottom: A window seat full of pillows provides a comfortable place to rest or read while keeping an eye on whatever is cooking.

FLEXIBLE SPACE FOR ENTERTAINING

This stunning kitchen was designed for two people with busy schedules who enjoy formal entertaining and who also have a growing family. Such diverse needs call for a multiple-use room that is also easy to maintain.

A family eating area separate from the formal dining room was created by adding a breakfast room to one end of the kitchen. It was part of a larger remodeling project and creates a link with the outdoor decks. Several elements help to keep the breakfast area distinct from the rest of the kitchen, including a vaulted ceiling of tongue-and-groove pine; huge windows and glass doors that open onto the deck; and natural wood walls, cabinets, and shelves. A wing wall near the refrigerator and an overhead beam also serve to define this area and break up the long space. Other features tie the areas together. The floor covering is the

Opposite: Serious thought went into every feature of this large kitchen. One important factor was the owners' desire to avoid doing any more remodeling any time soon. To accomplish this, they chose neutral colors and a classic look; installed durable, low-care ceramic tile on the walls; and selected the flooring for its durability.
Bottom: *The overhead pot-and-pan rack attached to the luminous ceiling was custom-made for this kitchen. It provides a convenient display and storage space.*

same in both rooms; and a short run of cabinets on both sides of the dividing wall makes for further continuity.

The dominant feature of this kitchen is the luminous ceiling. The grid was custom-made from 1 by 4 lumber and stained gray to match the cabinets. The use of boards instead of a conventional metal grid keeps the ceiling in scale with the large space. It is also higher than most ceilings—a full 8 feet off the floor—because the original ceiling was 9 feet high.

The luminous ceiling also helps to solve a major design problem: how to keep a long, narrow space from feeling like a tunnel. In this kitchen the tunnel effect would have been

exacerbated by the bright windows at one end. One solution in such a case is to open up one of the long walls with a continuous row of windows, but structural and visual constraints, as well as the need for wall space, made this impracticable. The luminous ceiling has the same effect as windows—it expands the space visually—only upwards instead of outwards. During the daytime it provides a strong balance to the bright natural light in the eating area.

This is a kitchen for serious cooks. Two identical refrigerators, with freezers below, provide ample space for storing salads and other dishes that can be prepared ahead of time.

There are double ovens, with a microwave-convection unit above and a conventional unit below, and an extra conventional oven mounted under the island countertop. The range area includes a commercial-style cooktop, a deep fryer, and a barbecue unit, which the owners use almost every day for grilling chicken or fish. The vent/hood has two high-capacity fans for maximum ventilation, and radiant-heat lamps over the wall racks to keep food warm. A bar sink in the island supplements the main sink. Storage space is maximized by roll-out shelves in the kick spaces and three pantry units with pull-out trays, spice racks, and other organizers.

The wood cabinets are stained gray to keep the space light and still reveal the subtle richness of the wood grain. The doors and drawers are full overlay, with a raised pattern that contributes to a sense of informal elegance. The wall cabinets extend full height to the 8-foot ceiling. Shorter cabinets were used on the two side walls, partly to accommodate the vent/hood and the espresso machine, and partly to expand the space visually. Full-length wall cabinets would have made it feel more narrow. The tops of the cabinets are trimmed with crown molding to tie them in with the ceiling grid.

Most of the countertops are covered with 3- by 4-inch brown tiles, which extend up the full height of the back splashes and walls. The grout matches the tiles. The counters are trimmed with half-round molding stained the same color as the cabinets. The island countertop is a slab of brownish rose marble. It is an ideal surface for rolling out pastry dough, but without special sealing it would be impractical for other uses because it stains easily.

Chosen both for good looks and for ease of care, the flooring is commercial grade vinyl in a neutral dark beige, with a pebbly texture.

An espresso machine was a must-have item on this family's needs list, so the necessary plumbing was specially installed above the countertop where it would sit.

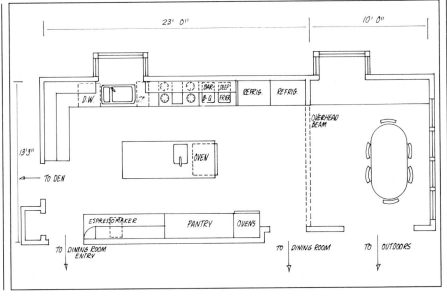

Professional Help

Kitchens are big business, and there are many sources to turn to for professional help with the design. How much professional advice you will need will depend on the scope of the project and on the extent to which you want to be involved. If you do your own design, you may want to hire someone on a consulting basis to go over your plan or to advise you about specific technical problems. You can also hire a professional to design everything, either for a set fee or for a percentage of the total project. The main thing is to be clear about what kind of help you need.

Besides someone who is reputable and enjoyable to work with, you are looking for someone who knows how to cook, understands food storage, knows the dynamics of an efficient work space, can produce accurate drawings and sketches, has up-to-the-minute information about products, can visualize floor plans, and appreciates the impact of three-dimensional spaces. He or she should also know how to work with color, have an eye for the subtleties of line and form, understand indoor lighting, know the local codes and practices, communicate well, be well organized, be realistic about budgets and costs, and be sensitive to your needs and desires. You may not find one person who has all of these qualifications. If you have expertise in some of these areas, hire a professional whose skills complement your own. If you hire more than one professional, get everyone involved early and be firm in setting who-does-what guidelines.

Satisfied customers are your best source for finding professional help. Ask family, friends, neighbors, and business associates for recommendations. Check the telephone directory for companies and individuals who specialize in kitchen remodeling. Visit kitchen showrooms and retail outlets and ask the personnel for the names of local professionals.

Architects

Licensed by the state, architects usually have a degree in architecture or engineering and have passed a rigorous series of exams. Although some architects specialize in kitchens, most have a broader scope of interest and expertise. Many architects will not only design the project but also supervise the construction. You will most likely need an architect if the project involves extensive remodeling, structural changes, or strict adherence to the unique architectural style of the house. Some architects plan the overall space and structural details and then collaborate with a kitchen specialist to complete the design. You may also want to hire an architect on an hourly consulting basis to analyze a structural change or solve a space-planning problem.

Kitchen Designers

As kitchen design has become more sophisticated, specialists have evolved who keep up-to-date on the latest products and trends. Some kitchen designers are affiliated with showrooms. Others are members of design firms or have independent practices. Those affiliated with showrooms may not offer you their services unless you buy the materials from them. Your choice of products is limited to the lines they carry, but the designer's service is usually free.

An independent designer can assist you through any or all phases of the project, from basic design through product selection to complete supervision of the construction. If you do your own design, consider having a designer consult with you on your plans. Fees are based on a package price, an hourly rate, or a percentage of the total project. If they are based on a markup of certain products, be aware that the designer may have a lead fee arrangement with a dealer and may not be recommending these products from an unbiased position.

Some kitchen designers are certified as CKD, which indicates membership in the Society of Certified Kitchen Designers, an agency of the National Kitchen and Bath Association (NKBA). Members are certified on the basis of education, experience, and a qualifying exam. Look for names followed by CKD in kitchen remodeling advertisements, or contact the association for a list of qualified professionals in your area.

National Kitchen and Bath Association
124 Main Street
Hackettstown, NJ 07840

Interior Designers

Traditionally, interior designers have been called in to coordinate colors, fabrics, lighting, furnishings, and other decorating features after the space has been planned, but today many of them will work with you in all stages of a remodeling project. You may find an interior designer who specializes in kitchens, or you may hire a generalist to help you to select colors and surface finishes or plan the lighting scheme. An interior designer also has access to items that are unusual or hard to find.

Contractors

Some contractors offer design services. A few are trained specifically in kitchen design, but most rely on their overall experience or general design skills. Some design-build firms have kitchen specialists on their staff. Contractors have a working knowledge of remodeling and a commitment to seeing the project through. A contractor may tend to design all kitchens the same way, but if you are familiar with his or her work and have a similar project in mind, hiring one contractor to do both design and construction can streamline the remodeling process.

PROJECT PLANNING

P roject planning is the transitional phase between designing a new kitchen and constructing it.

Professional contractors with years of experience in the field know that this is the most critical step of a project. They rarely start to do the hands-on work until all the planning is completed.

A home remodeling project is complex; it is made up of a series of different endeavors that must be coordinated. It's like producing a stage show while managing the theater and playing the lead role all at the same time. Remember, too, the show is being staged in your kitchen. Planning and preparation are essential if you want to avoid inconvenient and expensive downtime during construction. There are four steps to proper planning. They involve money, people, time, and the law. Estimating costs is a major concern of proper planning, as is choosing who will do which tasks. Once you've determined those two factors you'll need to schedule the project based on financial and personnel priorities. Obtaining permits is a part of the construction process that must be addressed before any work begins. The guidelines presented here should help you to escape the pitfalls common to a poorly planned project.

Both the design and the construction of this beautiful kitchen remodeling were executed by the homeowners, neither of whom is a construction professional, over the course of a year. Their attention to detail provided a room that is aesthetically pleasing and suits their life-style.

ESTIMATING COSTS

One of the most important steps in construction begins long before you pound a nail: estimating the cost. It is also the most difficult step. An accurate estimate for any construction project requires a detailed set of plans and specifications. Do not rely on your own preliminary plans, on a designer's estimate of projected costs, or on any contractor's price that is not a firm bid based on the final plans.

Plans and specifications should include all proposed changes to the structure; the locations of all plumbing, electrical, heating, and ventilating devices; the type of flooring, finish wall, countertop, and ceiling materials; window and door specifications; cabinet sizes and finishes; and the makes and models of all appliances. These specifications enable you and the contractor, subcontractors, suppliers, and consultants to account for every detail. Because the project involves remodeling an existing kitchen, plan too on surprises and cost overruns.

Getting Contractors' Bids

If you are hiring a general contractor or a group of subcontractors, their bids will be the estimate. Be sure that you know exactly what is and is not included in each bid. For instance, who will be responsible for removing debris? For purchasing and installing appliances? For painting? If your plans do not specify such details as type of tile, brand of sink faucet, or type of cabinet hardware, clarify whether the bids include a certain allowance for these items or whether they assume that cheap materials will be used. In the latter case you will have to pay the difference if you want

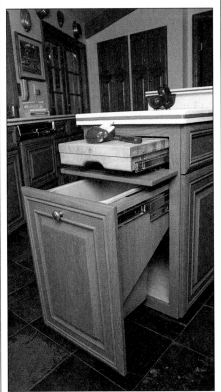

Anticipate your food preparation needs when you plan your new kitchen. This homeowner-designed combination pull-out chopping board and trash receptacle takes advantage of the corner of the kitchen island.

more expensive items. Also, try to identify where problems may arise, or where you may decide to opt for add-ons that would require a change order. This too involves extra expense. Examples might be changing a single patio door to a pair of French doors, discovering an inadequate roof structure if you plan to raise the ceiling, or having to update the electrical service to accommodate the extra circuit loads. In order to assure an accurate comparison, be sure that each person doing an estimate is given the same information.

Doing Your Own Estimate

If you are acting as your own general contractor, you will have to do the cost estimate yourself. The most reliable way to estimate the cost of a job is to break it down into separate phases, itemize the materials and labor costs for each phase, total them up, and add a reasonable contingency factor to the total.

If you plan to hire subcontractors for some of the work, use their bids as estimates for those phases. For the rest of the project, use a work sheet similar to the one on page 65, basing it on your plans and on the construction information in the fourth chapter. To price materials, make a complete list and shop around at various suppliers. Labor will be harder to estimate. Even if you are doing all the work yourself, you should estimate the time, so that you will have goals to aim for.

Discovering Hidden Costs

Most of the costs of a remodeling project are predictable. They are the features in the plans that you spend a great deal of time deciding on: the extent of the remodeling, the surface materials, the appliances, and the accessories. However, there are hidden costs as well. These costs are easy to overlook, and they can add up significantly over the course of a long

project. Spend some time during the planning phase thinking about hidden costs that may affect your budget. These are typical examples:
□ Permit fees
□ Employer expenses for hiring labor (taxes, Workers' Compensation, insurance)
□ Tools, either to buy or to rent
□ Sharpening or replacing blades
□ Power cords and lights
□ Safety equipment: goggles, gloves, dust masks, painter's masks
□ Vehicle mileage, wear and tear
□ Increased use of telephone and utilities
□ Debris box rental or dump fees
□ Tarps or plastic sheeting to cover supplies
□ Resizing a gas line to meet increased demand
□ Rewiring the whole house "while we're at it"
□ Matching obsolete finish materials, such as moldings
□ Inability to recycle existing materials as originally planned
□ Patching the roof or siding around new vents, outlets, windows, or skylights
□ Buying or renting ladders or scaffolding
□ Enlarging a deck or porch to accommodate new doors
□ Delivery charges for materials
□ Insulating exterior walls you hadn't intended to open up
□ Repair of accidental damage to carpets, doorways, and landscaping
□ New furniture, cookware, and other accessories
□ Cost of dining out while the kitchen is out of service

Cutting Costs

The cost estimate should include a contingency factor, usually 5 to 10 percent, to take care of cost overruns. When you have a grand total, you may need to adjust it to fit your budget. Before you revise the design accordingly, consider the following ways to cut costs.

Shop for Values

Look for package deals by buying as much of the materials list in one place as you can. Bring a set of plans with you, so the dealer knows you mean business. Prepare as complete a materials list as possible, down to the nails and fasteners. Read advertisements; look for sales, such as inventory clearances or seasonal specials. Consider buying sale appliances and materials and storing them until you can install them.

Work Yourself

You won't always save money by doing your own work, but by concentrating on labor-intensive tasks such as demolition, finishing wallboard, painting, installing tile, and cleanup, you can save.

Work in Phases

One way to budget is to schedule the work over several years. This may be difficult with a kitchen, but if the project also involves adding an outdoor deck, a separate laundry room, or a large breakfast room, you may be able to wait to add these components until the budget is healthier.

Change Your Specifications

Save money by eliminating the most expensive item, or exchange it for a less expensive version. Exchanging a commercial-style range for a standard model or a slab stone countertop for a laminate version may make it possible to keep everything else you want.

Scale Down

It may be impossible to adjust the size of the kitchen—it is probably small enough as it is—but consider keeping more of the existing fixtures than you had planned, or not making unnecessary structural changes such as raising the ceiling.

Move

This is a drastic solution, to say the least, but be realistic. Investigate the real-estate market and make sure there are no bargains out there that you weren't aware of.

Sample Cost Breakdown of Sink Installation

Task	Materials	Tools	Labor
Cut out hole	—	Pencil, drill, saber saw	¼ hour
Install shutoff valves	2 valves 2 escutcheons	Tubing cutter, 2 wrenches	¼ hour
Install disposer drain fitting	Disposer, putty	Screwdriver	½ hour
Install faucet and sprayer	Faucet, caulk, sprayer	Basin wrench, open-end wrench	¼ hour
Install sink	Sink, rim, caulk, clips	Screwdriver	¼ hour
Hook up water supply	Supply risers	Basin wrench, open-end wrench	¼ hour
Install disposer	Cord, plug, elbow	Screwdriver, wrench	½ hour
Hook up drain	P-trap	Adjustable pliers	¼ hour
Install instant hot water	Unit, flex tubing, caulk, screws	Wrenches, screwdriver, tubing cutter	½ hour

ASSIGNING TASKS

Before you engage professional help, decide to what extent you will be involved in the project. After reading this book you will have a good idea of what skills, tools, and experience are required for each stage of a kitchen remodeling. There is no guarantee that doing any of the work yourself will save you money, especially if you put a value on your time. But if you enjoy physical work, have safe and reliable work habits, and take pleasure in shaping your own living space, you should do as much of the work as possible. These guidelines will help you to assess your readiness for involvement.

Managing the Project

You may want to manage the job yourself and hire subcontractors—carpenters, plumbers, electricians, wallboard finishers, cabinet installers, painters, and tilers—to do the actual work. Although you will be hiring professionals, you will still have certain responsibilities.

To be an effective project manager you must be well organized, persistent, and clear about the details of your design. You must be available to spend long hours on the telephone and at the job. You must be confident about handling money, and you must make payments promptly and keep a budget. You must be comfortable negotiating with subcontractors and suppliers. You must be articulate, firm, and patient, and be willing both to be friendly and to stay out of the way. Finally, you must be able to direct all inquiries, complaints, or compliments to the person with whom you signed the relevant contract.

Subcontractors depend on accurate scheduling. If your job is not ready when they arrive, they must reschedule it: You may not see them again for several days or even weeks and you may be charged for their downtime. You must stay on top of every phase of construction and inform all the subcontractors if you expect any delays.

If you plan to hire salaried workers, you must be willing to take on the responsibilities of an employer. These include reporting wages to the IRS, withholding state and federal taxes, paying the employer's share of such taxes, and carrying a Workers' Compensation insurance policy.

Performing a Trade

If you are experienced in a construction trade, such as carpentry or wiring, or with a material, such as wallboard, paint, or tile, and if you have access to the proper tools, you should consider doing that portion of the project yourself and hiring help to do the other parts. If you will be performing a trade but not acting as the project manager, you must be willing to be assigned as subcontractor by the contractor. You must make yourself available whenever necessary, have your materials ready, and complete the work as scheduled.

If you work in the trades and have friends who work in the trades, you may be able to barter some of the construction work. Consider exchanging your skills for theirs on construction projects in each other's homes. A barter should be negotiated like any other estimate, and a contract should be written for everyone's protection.

Here are some other ways to help cut costs.
□ Do the work of the most highly paid professionals (usually plumbers and electricians) if you have the skills.
□ Do tasks with a high labor cost, such as wallboard finishing, insulating, and painting.
□ Do small jobs that would take a subcontractor less than half a day to perform, such as installing resilient sheet flooring.

Doing General Labor

Just about everyone has the skills to perform general labor on a kitchen remodeling project. You must be available on short notice, assist with menial tasks, be in good physical condition, and be willing to get dirty. In order to save money by hiring yourself for these jobs, there must be a significant amount of demolition, hauling, or simple alterations that you can do before the professionals take over. Be sure that the contract clearly specifies which tasks are the contractor's responsibility and which are yours. General labor offers teenagers an excellent chance to earn money and learn a basic marketable skill. You might consider scheduling the remodeling during a school vacation, so that your children can work on the project.

Doing Everything Yourself

If you enjoy working on your home and have time to devote to learning and performing construction tasks, you can do all of the work yourself. Smaller remodeling and refacing projects can often be completed over a long weekend. Longer jobs will require careful planning in order to avoid long delays while you are busy living your normal life. Work out a schedule and stick to it.

If you plan to do all of the work yourself you should be aware of the risks. If you work on the project while you pursue your regular profession, and do all of the construction on evenings and weekends, it will take much longer than it would if you hired professionals. Inspectors and some suppliers are available only during regular business hours, and someone will have to be home during the week to work with them.

Hiring Professional Help

Finding the right contractor is as important as choosing cabinets or estimating costs. You may already be working with a design firm that offers contracting or installation services, or you may have selected a contractor whose work you know. Otherwise you should solicit the names of contractors from your designer, suppliers, and friends, or from trade associations such as the National Association of the Remodeling Industry (NARI) or the Remodelers Council of the National Association of Home Builders (NAHB).

Selecting a Contractor

The time-honored way to select a contractor is through competitive bidding, but kitchen remodeling does not always lend itself to fixed bids because there are so many variables. Going with the lowest bid does not guarantee that you will be satisfied with the quality of the service. Provide detailed plans and specifications; distinguish clearly between your role and that of the contractor; and set clear terms for change orders to handle contingencies. A change order is a written agreement between the owner and the contractor directing adjustments or additions to the original plans once construction has begun. Contingencies are the surprises that crop up along the way. All this will help to reduce the number of variables and make fixed-bid contracts go more smoothly. You may also consider negotiating a time-and-materials contract. The advantages of

such a contract are that you pay only the actual cost of the job, and you get more attentive service. The disadvantages are that you don't know exactly how much the job will cost until it is finished, and you don't know what it would have cost to have another contractor do the same job. The main thing to recognize is that you are shopping for a service, not a product, such as an automobile.

If you solicit fixed bids, the following guidelines will help you to observe the correct etiquette.

☐ Do not solicit a formal bid process if you already have a contractor in mind. Just negotiate directly.

☐ In your initial phone call to each contractor, describe the project briefly and mention that complete plans are available.

☐ Have ready a list of questions about the contractor's experience with similar jobs, method of scheduling construction, and references.

☐ Check references by visiting job sites and completed projects. Ask previous clients if they were satisfied with the contractor's performance and attitude.

☐ Narrow your choices down to three or four people and provide each one with a complete set of plans.

☐ Set a firm date for receiving bids. Allow at least two weeks if the project is a complete remodeling that will involve several subcontractors.

☐ Specify what materials and labor you yourself intend to provide.

☐ If a bidder requests clarification or information, answer the request in writing. Send a copy of your answer, labeled Addendum, to each bidder.

☐ Use the same process to notify bidders of any changes you make in the plans after they have been submitted.

☐ Along with the price quote, request a copy of the contract form that the bidder expects you to sign, as well as the bidder's credit references.

☐ Review the bids and forms.

The selection of a contractor should be based on several factors: personal rapport, experience with similar jobs, references and recommendations, schedules (yours and the

contractor's), and cost. The low bid is not necessarily the one to choose. It may indicate sloppy work, inadequate supervision, or serious oversights. It may also lead to costly changes later on. It is unethical to negotiate simultaneously with two contractors after you have received their bids, or to invite another contractor to compete after the bidding process has closed. Remember to notify all parties of your choice and of the winning bid price, and thank them for taking the time to bid.

Signing the Contracts

Always insist on a well-written contract. It does not have to be elaborate; since most contractors already have their own contract form, you can use that as a starting point. Not all of the following provisions will apply to your particular situation, but a good contract should include these points.

☐ Reference to the construction documents as the criteria of performance.

☐ Stipulation that all permits are to be obtained by the contractor and all work be done according to code.

☐ Specified start and completion dates and a detailed schedule.

☐ Clear delineations of the contractor's duties and of your own.

☐ Specification of the work that you intend to perform yourself.

☐ A list of all materials or fixtures that you will be supplying.

☐ A payment schedule corresponding to key completion dates.

☐ A provision for the contractor to supply lien releases from all subcontractors and suppliers before final payment is made.

☐ Requirements for final payment, including final inspection by the building inspection department, and a certificate of completion signed by you and the architect (if applicable). Maintain a 30-day waiting period prior to payment to ensure that you are satisfied with the work.

☐ A specific procedure for handling change orders.

☐ Specific procedures for communication when more than one professional is involved.

☐ A method for resolving disputes

SCHEDULING THE PROJECT

Y ou may not discover how to get more hours into the day, but following a detailed time line will help you to negotiate contracts, schedule your own time, and estimate the date of completion. The first step in preparing a time line is to establish the sequence of construction. The actual sequence will vary from job to job, but the following example is typical of most kitchen remodeling projects that do not involve an addition or other major structural changes.

Developing a Time Line

Once you have established the sequence of construction, estimate the time needed to complete each step. Transfer the information to a calendar or make the sequence list into a time line by writing in the starting and ending date for each item. Some jobs can be done simultaneously, while others must be done in sequence. Contact suppliers to find out the lead times for various materials, such as cabinets, appliances, floor coverings, and tile, so that you will know when to order them. Some will take only a few days; others may take months if they must be shipped from overseas or made to order. Adjust the time line to coordinate it with the delivery of materials.

Preconstruction
1. Complete the design.
2. Obtain bids or work up an estimate.
3. Prepare a time line.
4. Arrange for financing.
5. Hire a contractor or subcontractors as needed.
6. Order materials and fixtures with delayed delivery times.
7. Obtain permits.
8. Establish a temporary kitchen.
9. Arrange for removal of debris and storage of materials.

Demolition
10. Clear out the kitchen.
11. Seal off the kitchen from the rest of the house.
12. Remove appliances and plumbing fixtures.
13. Remove countertops, cabinets, and other built-ins.
14. Remove trim and moldings.
15. Remove floor covering if necessary.
16. Remove lights and electrical fixtures.
17. Remove wall and ceiling materials, such as paneling, plaster, or wallboard, as needed.

Preparing the Space
18. Remove or alter walls; shore up bearing walls.
19. Repair subfloor if necessary.
20. Complete rough framing for alterations, new walls, soffits, windows, doors, and skylights.
21. Install new windows and exterior doors.
22. Install duct work for range hood and heating system.
23. Alter or install rough plumbing.
24. Alter or install rough wiring.
25. Get preliminary inspections.
26. Install insulation and get it inspected if required.
27. Repair, replace, or install wall surfaces; apply finish.
28. Install door and window trim, except where it will be fitted around cabinets.

29. Paint ceiling, walls, and trim.
30. Install flooring, including underlayment. (Some flooring is installed at the end of the project, however.)
31. Install interior doors.

Installing Finishes and Fixtures
32. Install cabinets, cabinet trim, and other storage units.
33. Install countertops and back splashes.
34. Install baseboards and remaining (pre-painted) trim pieces.
35. Install sink, garbage disposer, and plumbing fixtures.
36. Apply wallcoverings.
37. Install light fixtures and finish installing electrical fixtures.
38. Install range hood, dishwasher, cooktop, oven, and microwave.
39. Install overhead racks, towel bars, window coverings, and other accessories.
40. Install flooring, if this has not already been done.
41. Install refrigerator, slide-in range, trash compactor, and other movable appliances or fixtures.

Cleanup
42. Clean up and remove trash.
43. Touch up paint and stains.
44. Test electrical system, plumbing, and appliances.
45. Obtain final inspections.
46. Move in.

Now you have an estimated time of completion and a set of milestones along the way for checking your progress. If you hire a contractor, you may have to coordinate the time line with his or her schedule as well.

Opposite: If you plan to hire professionals to do some or all of your construction, coordinating these various workers will be an important aspect of the planning process. Three different experts built, marbleized, and installed the cabinets in this exciting kitchen.

Obtaining Financing

Unless you are one of that rare breed who are able to pay for a new kitchen out of ready cash, you will have to do some financial planning to determine your budget and arrange for financing. Most lenders require the following information, and it will also help you to set a realistic budget. You will need to know:

☐ Your total net worth
☐ Anticipated new expenses, such as a baby, a car, or college tuition
☐ Your expected cash flow during the design and construction phases (and afterwards, if you obtain a loan)
☐ Your borrowing power

To figure your net worth, follow these steps.
1. Total your assets (cash; savings accounts; checking accounts; stocks; bonds; securities; surrender value of life insurance; market value of real estate, automobiles, furnishings, jewelry, pension funds).
2. Total your liabilities (real-estate loans, accounts and contracts payable, installment loans).
3. Subtract total liabilities from total assets to find your net worth. This is the amount of assets you can liquidate or pledge as security for a loan.

To figure your average net monthly cash flow, follow these steps.
1. Total your current monthly income (net wages, investment income, monthly value of health and other benefits).
2. Total your current monthly expenses (mortgages, auto loans, property taxes, insurance payments, installment and credit card payments, living expenses).
3. Subtract expenses from income to get current net monthly cash flow.
4. Project your net monthly cash flow for the next five years by adding any expected new income and subtracting any anticipated new expenses. Be sure to include new monthly expenses that will be incurred by the improvements to the

kitchen, such as higher insurance premiums or property taxes.
5. Average your current and projected net monthly cash flow to get your estimated net monthly cash flow. This will give you a realistic idea of how much money will be available every month to pay back a new loan. A remodeled kitchen will have a positive impact on the value of your home. You should consider the value of your home, both now and after you have remodeled the kitchen, to help you to arrive at a realistic budget. Consult with a local real-estate agent or hire a professional appraiser.

Once you have determined your budget and have estimated the cost of the new kitchen, obtain the financing so that funds will be available by the time you begin construction.

Opposite: *Special needs must be incorporated into every room design. A low countertop with plenty of undercounter space provides an ample food preparation area for a wheelchair-bound cook.*
Top: *Kitchens that will be used by several cooks must accommodate the needs of each. Pull-out chopping boards positioned lower than usual make food preparation easier for helpful children and for people who are wheelchair-bound.*

PURSUING PERMITS

I n most communities you will be required to obtain a building permit before starting construction. Usually the homeowner is allowed to apply for the permit, but in some communities permits may be issued only to licensed contractors. You can probably have the permit issued immediately if you are making only minor alterations to an existing kitchen. If you are making a large addition or major structural changes, local authorities may be required to check the plans, a process that could take several days.

Separate permits are customarily issued for the building, plumbing, electrical, and mechanical stages of the project.

Besides complying with the law, you gain several other advantages when you obtain a permit. It validates any work you have done that affects the resale value of the house. It decreases the possibility that an insurance company would refuse a claim against fire or other damages of dubious origin. It gives you an incentive to plan the project thoroughly, and a sense of pride in your work. Finally, and most importantly, codes and permits exist to ensure that you and your family will be living in a safe home.

Handling Inspections

The building permit will include a schedule of inspections. Generally, all work must be inspected before it is covered up. A final inspection is made after everything is hooked up and ready to go. A typical schedule of inspections appears below.

If you hire a contractor, he or she will call for inspections and be responsible for answering questions. However, you may have to make arrangements to let the inspector onto the premises if the contractor cannot be there to do so.

The local building inspection department can tell you what codes pertain to your work and can answer specific questions about code requirements. However, staff members cannot advise you how to do the work. If you have done the work yourself and are not sure whether it will meet code, hire a professional who is familiar with the local codes to take a look at it before the inspection is made.

The Final Plan

Although it may have taken months to consider all the design factors and to refine the plan, be prepared to make some adjustments after the plans are checked and in order to obtain all the proper permits. However, the better prepared your plans are, the smoother the plan-checking process will go.

For inspection and permit purposes, prepare a package that contains the final drawings and specifications. These include a detailed floor plan, elevations, and a list of all the materials and fixtures that you will use. A file folder case or closeable three-ring binder work well to hold all the paper work. You may need only a floor plan to obtain a permit for a simple remodeling, but you will need the elevations and structural drawings for more complex projects. You'll need them anyway during construction, so having all these materials in one place will make your management job easier.

Inspection Schedule

Job	Work to Be Checked	Time of Inspection
Foundation	Trench, forms, rebar	Before concrete is poured
Under floor	Floor framing, utility lines	Before subfloor is installed
Framing	Grade & size of lumber, spans, connections, sheathing	Before walls are insulated or covered up
Rough plumbing	Pipe sizes, fittings, pressure test	Before framing is inspected or walls covered up
Rough wiring	Wire size, boxes, bends	Before framing is inspected or walls covered up
Rough mechanical	Ducts, flues, clearances, gas lines	Before framing is inspected or walls covered up
Insulation	Thickness, joints, cracks	Before wallboard is applied
Interior walls	Wallboard nailing pattern (may not be required)	Before joints are taped
Final inspection	Electrical fixtures, plumbing fixtures, window glass, stairs	After completion

Top: *Artwork should not be left out of the kitchen. Plan the decorative elements of your remodeling project in coordination with the other steps in the construction process. This neon sculpture was commissioned especially to be the centerpiece of this kitchen.*

Bottom: *Knocking down the wall between the original kitchen and laundry gives this kitchen a wide-open feeling and plenty of counter space. Undercounter washer and dryer are within easy reach of the back door and allow for a wide clothes-folding area. The communication center, placed in the middle of the new space, includes an undercounter telephone and desk drawers.*

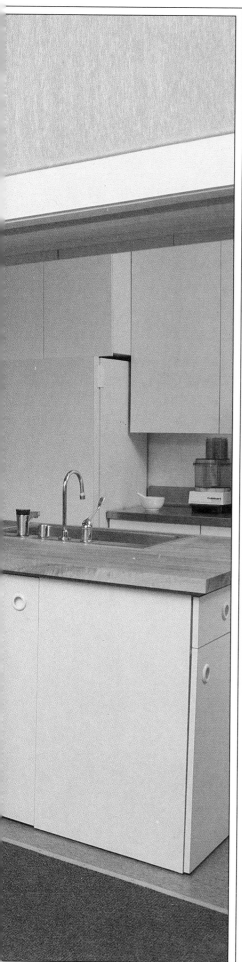

CONSTRUCTION GUIDE

Remodeling a kitchen is a demanding project that requires careful preparation, timely coordination, and accurate work. It involves many different skills and a variety of materials and fixtures. It may also mean having to get along without a kitchen, perhaps for several weeks. However, the satisfaction of working on your own home and the reward of a beautiful kitchen should offset any inconveniences. This chapter will guide you through each phase of the project. Before you can begin the remodeling, you must first demolish the existing kitchen and then prepare the new space. The order in which you install various elements varies with the design, but cabinets, countertops, sinks and faucets, lights, windows, flooring, and appliances must each be installed in turn. Tasks unique to kitchen remodeling are presented in step-by-step detail. Techniques common to all remodeling are summarized. Jobs are presented in the normal sequence of construction, but this can vary greatly. Read about every phase of the project before you begin remodeling so that you can sequence the work correctly.

Fifteen feet were added to the rear of this home in order to accommodate the large, gourmet-theme kitchen and adjoining dining room. The homeowner uses this area very often, both for entertaining and for teaching professional cooking classes.

DISMANTLING THE OLD KITCHEN

It may be encouraging to know that demolition requires more common sense than technical skill, and knowledge of a few fundamentals rather than a specific answer to every question that comes up. It is easy to think of demolition as sledgehammer work, but in fact it seldom requires brute strength.

You will be most successful at dismantling the existing kitchen if you think of it as finesse work. Take things a step at a time and nibble away at the kitchen rather than demolishing it all at once. Even if you are moving walls or making structural changes, planning the job carefully, having the proper tools, and developing safe work habits will do more to ensure a successful project than will actual skills and techniques.

Because dismantling is a job that depends on logic rather than on strength, and because it requires more time than skill, it is an excellent project to do yourself, even if you plan to hire help for the rest of your construction.

Dismantling is generally done in the following order: appliances and fixtures, countertops, cabinets, ceilings and walls, and flooring. Removal of electrical fixtures, plumbing, duct work, and other structural elements will depend on the extent of the remodeling plans. Read through this section to get an idea of how much time the various procedures will take.

If the kitchen project entails adding on new space, the shell for the addition can usually be framed up and closed in before you open up the wall and disrupt your present kitchen. Just be sure that the door or opening in the new addition is large enough to accomodate the removal of old cabinets and debris and the delivery of bulky items.

Creating a Temporary Kitchen

Make preparations for a temporary kitchen well before the start of demolition. Choose a space that will minimize the inconvenience you'll have to endure; do not impose more austerity than is necessary. Locate the temporary kitchen near a bathroom, laundry, or wet bar or other sink. Avoid setting it up within a bathroom unless there is another bathroom for normal use. Provide a countertop near the sink. Also consider proximity to a comfortable eating area. Arrange space for the old refrigerator, storage shelves or cabinets, and a generous countertop (separate from the table where you plan to eat).

Set up cooking appliances—hot plates and microwave and toaster ovens—in a well-ventilated area, away from curtains and other flammable objects. If you are planning to buy a new microwave for the new kitchen, consider buying it early so you can use it in your temporary kitchen. If the weather is good, use your outdoor barbecue and camp stove to cook hot meals.

Be wary of overloading circuits in rooms that were not intended to serve as kitchens. Plan to use only one or two appliances at the same time. Be sure that three-prong cords are plugged into grounded outlets.

When you clear out your kitchen, pack up everything you're not planning to use in your temporary kitchen, label the cartons clearly, and store them in a convenient place.

If your home is too crowded to set up an adequate temporary kitchen, consider borrowing a recreational vehicle for a month or two and cooking there. You might also consider eating out (many restaurants offer early-bird specials), living elsewhere, or (if you are not doing the construction work yourself) scheduling a long trip. Think ahead and anticipate the discomforts before they surprise you. With a little planning, some minor inconvenience, and a lot of good humor, you will manage.

Tools and Equipment

Dismantling goes much more smoothly with the right tools. Most tasks can be done with basic hand tools, but be sure they are of good quality. Do not hesitate to obtain any tool that is necessary; there is no substitute for the right tool.

Depending on the scope of the work, you will need a hammer with a ripping claw, a utility knife with extra blades, a flat pry bar, a 3-inch-wide putty knife, a minihacksaw, a small handsaw, an adjustable wrench, adjustable pliers, an assortment of screwdrivers, and a simple voltage tester. More specialized tools include needle-nose pliers, side cutters, end cutters, a large wrecking bar, a brickset, pipe wrenches, a flat shovel for loading debris, and a wheelbarrow for carrying equipment in and debris out. Power tools that are helpful include a reciprocating saw with both long and short blades, a 3/8-inch drill with screwdriver bits (a cordless drill is a plus), and a circular saw.

Make plans ahead of time for dealing with debris. Even a modest kitchen project can generate a mountain of trash debris in a short time. Your options are to haul everything away as you remove it, which requires a pickup truck, trailer, or large station wagon; to create a debris pile in an out-of-the-way but accessible location and have it hauled away at the end of the job; or to rent a debris box and toss the trash into it as you go. Most debris box services require pickup within a short time (usually a week), so you will have to complete all demolition within that time. Remember that there will be more debris from later phases of the project as well.

Safety and Security

Always put safety first. Construction can be hazardous, but safe work habits, an uncluttered job site, basic safety equipment, and awareness of your own limitations will minimize the chance of an injury. Have gloves, safety goggles, dust masks, and a protective hat available at all times, and remember to use them. Get a tetanus shot if you have not had one recently.

Observe safe work habits. Try not to force things when dismantling them; let your tools do the work. Wear a hard hat whenever someone is working above you or whenever you are removing ceiling materials. Be aware of safe lifting techniques: Use your legs instead of your back, keep a firm footing, and avoid twisting your back as you lift or hold heavy objects. Make it a practice to remove nails from boards or to bend the nails over before you toss the boards on a debris pile. Wear a dust mask or respirator during dusty operations. If you encounter asbestos (found in some flooring materials, flue pipes, and ceiling textures), seek professional assistance. Read directions carefully for solvents, adhesives, and any other volatile product that is potentially flammable. Avoid working when you are tired or mentally fatigued and be extra alert toward the end of the day. Injuries often occur around quitting time.

Use power tools with care. Make sure safety guards are intact, use goggles, and do not wear loose clothing. Be sure power cords and tools are in good condition and are properly grounded. Keep saw blades and drill bits sharp.

Turn off all utilities before you work on any appliance or tear into a wall. Most gas or propane appliances have shutoff valves behind them, but find out how to operate the main valve to the house in case you need to turn it off quickly. However, once you turn off the gas to the whole house, the pilot lights for all the remaining appliances, such as the furnace and the water heater, will have to be relit, unless they have electronic ignition devices. It is a good idea to have a service representative from the utility company come out to help you turn the gas back on whenever you disconnect any gas appliances.

Turn off circuit breakers or disconnect fuses that serve wires in the area where you will be working. Cover the breaker with tape to warn other people that it was turned off intentionally. Use a voltage tester to check that there is no current remaining in electrical outlets or fixtures that you plan to work on. If you are uncertain about disconnecting utilities, get professional help.

You may want to notify your insurance carrier about the construction work that is being done on your home—especially if you plan to enlist the help of family and friends. Be sure that your policy will cover any accidents that may occur.

Demolition work often involves the removal of doors, windows, and even entire walls. Plan a way to secure these openings at the end of each workday.

One of the most important concerns is keeping dust and debris out of the rest of the house. Before you begin work, seal off all doorways and passageways that dust can penetrate. Shut any doors that can be left closed and apply duct tape around the edges, especially at the bottom. If, however, the door cannot be taken out of service, apply duct tape along the bottom of the door on both sides. Attach the tape just to the door, not to the floor. It will act as a dust sweep as you open and close the door. Passageways without doors can be sealed with 4-millimeter plastic sheeting. Attach the plastic to the ceiling with a 1 by 2 or similar board, driving nails into ceiling joists. Use another board to anchor the bottom.

Now, with the kitchen cleared out and sealed off from the rest of the house, you are ready to begin.

Removing Fixtures

Freestanding appliances can simply be unplugged and carted away. It is worth the expense to rent an appliance dolly for a few hours if you have to move them far or take them up or down stairs.

Drop-in Range

Open the oven door and look for the screws or similar fasteners that attach the unit to the side cabinets. Unscrew them and get someone to help you lift the range out far enough to unplug it. If it is a gas range, turn off the gas valve and disconnect the supply pipe anywhere on the range side of the valve. Then lift out the unit.

Wall Oven

The electrical or gas connections are probably in the cabinet below the unit. Unplug the cord from the wall receptacle. If the electrical connection is directly wired with no plug, deaden the circuit at the breaker panel; remove the cover plate from the wall; and disconnect the wires inside the wall box. Check each wire with a voltage tester before working on it. After disconnecting the wires, cap the exposed wires in the wall box with wire nuts. If the oven is gas, unplug any electrical cords and disconnect the gas line as described above for a gas range.

To remove the oven unit, open the doors and remove any screws holding the unit to the cabinet. Then slide the oven forward, lift it down onto a dolly, and cart it away.

Cooktop

The electrical or gas connection will probably be in the cabinet below or to one side of the cooktop. If the unit is electric, disconnect it the same way as you would a wall oven. If it is gas, shut off the gas valve and disconnect the flexible tubing from the valve. Be sure to plug the outlet of the valve after removing the cooktop. To remove the cooktop, unscrew the fasteners that hold it to the countertop. Then lift up the unit and take it away.

Range Hood

Make sure the electricity is off. You will probably find the electrical connection beneath the easily removable light diffuser or filter panel. Disconnect the wires, and cap the wires coming from the wall with wire nuts. Keep any pairs of wires together and cap each single wire separately. The bare copper wire is the ground wire and needs no cap.

Open the cabinet doors above the hood to see how the vent connects to the exhaust duct. If you find a round metal collar, unsnap it. If you find a band of silver or gray duct tape around the connection, remove it. Look for any screws in the duct joint and take them out. You may find flanges that hold down a sheet-metal box custom-made to fit your hood-to-duct connection. Remove the nails or screws holding it in place.

Look up inside the hood to see where the mounting screws attach it to the upper cabinets. Remove them from the mounting brackets or holes and lift the hood out and down. Be careful. It may drop suddenly if you are not supporting it while you remove the mounting screws.

Garbage Disposer

Unplug the disposer or, if it is wired directly into the wall, turn off the circuit breaker, remove the cover plate, disconnect the wiring, and cap the wires left in the wall box. Be sure the circuit breaker for the dishwasher is also turned off before working on any wires.

Place a bucket under the P-trap and loosen the slip nuts with channel-type pliers, a pipe wrench, or a special spud wrench until the trap drops free. If the trap won't come free, cut it with a hacksaw.

Remove the garbage disposer after disconnecting the drain hose from the dishwasher or air gap. Be sure to support the disposer while you are disconnecting it; it will drop suddenly. Leave the bucket under the drain in case the faucet is accidentally turned on.

Sink and Faucet

Turn off the water at the shutoff valves below the sink and disconnect the supply tubes from the valves. If there are no shutoff valves, turn off the water at the main valve for the house, disconnect the pipes at the sink, and cap them before turning the water back on. Have a bucket handy to catch any water trapped in the pipes. (By opening the sink faucet before shutting off the water and leaving a faucet open at a lower point elsewhere in the house—bathtub, outdoor faucet, downstairs sink—you can drain the pipes before you disconnect them.)

If you want to remove the faucet to save it, detach the supply tubes by loosening the connecting nuts from below. Use a basin wrench, a special tool with a long arm for reaching into tight spaces. Then loosen and disconnect the nuts that hold the faucet to the sink and pull the faucet out from above. Remove the P-trap or any trap arms that are still attached to the sink.

The sequence for removing a sink mounted in a countertop varies with the type of installation. If the sink is recessed under tiles, you will have to chip out the trim tiles from around the rim to free it. Most cast-iron sinks are held in place with adhesive. Simply pry up on the rim and lift out the sink. The sink is heavy, so get help. Lightweight sinks, such as those made of stainless steel and enameled steel, can be left in place and removed with the countertop as a unit. They are held in place with clips mounted below the rim. To remove the sink, loosen the clips with a screwdriver until you can jiggle them free. Then lift out the sink from above.

Old-fashioned sinks mounted to the wall are attached to a heavy wall bracket with clamps. Remove the clamps so the sink can be lifted off the bracket. These sinks are heavy, so get help and lift carefully. If the sink does not lift easily, you may need to loosen it from below.

Removing Countertops

Most countertops are plywood or particleboard with the finish surface applied to the top, or slabs of solid material, such as synthetic marble or butcher block. These countertops can be removed as a unit. They are generally fastened to the cabinets from below with screws. However, some installations must be broken up in order to be removed. In any case try to remove as much of the countertop as possible in one piece. How well you succeed will depend on how heavy the countertop is, how it's attached, and whether or not you plan to save the base cabinets. Be careful! Wear goggles and heavy gloves—broken tile, laminate, and slab is sharp. Take out the sink, if necessary. Remove all the drawers from the base cabinets and take off doors as needed to give access to the fasteners.

Removing Cabinets

Cabinets can be attached in several different ways. They can be nailed or screwed to the wall, to the soffit above, or to each other.

Cabinets built on site are difficult to salvage, since they must be removed a piece at a time in the opposite order to that in which they were built. Take them apart with a hammer, pry bar, and saw and save the good lumber. Older cabinets were sometimes built into the wall itself; you may have to demolish them along with part of the wall. Metal cabinets are attached to the wall on hangers. Lift the cabinet out and away from the wall at the bottom and then lift it off the hangers. Remove the hangers from the wall.

Cabinets installed as prefabricated units are the easiest to remove. They can be saved to use for storage.

Whether you start with the wall cabinets or the base cabinets is a matter of choice. If you start with the wall units, you can use the base units for support. If you start with the base units, it will be easier to reach the wall units.

Removing Wall and Ceiling Materials

Not all projects require the removal of wall or ceiling materials. You may be able to cover the old surfaces. If the walls and ceiling are in poor shape, or if changes will be made in the structure, wiring, or plumbing, then at least some of these materials must be removed. If you are providing access only for small changes in the plumbing and wiring, you can wait until later to make the openings.

Removing wall and ceiling materials can be time-consuming and messy, but it is not particularly complicated. Wear gloves, goggles, a dust mask, and a hard hat when removing plaster or wallboard. If the kitchen is being completely renovated with extensive changes in the structure, wiring, and plumbing, gut out the room to the wall studs and ceiling framing. It is tempting to leave small sections of wall or ceiling material intact, but they are seldom worth saving unless you can salvage a whole wall. Patching into the smaller sections is tedious, and you will probably need to get behind them to work on the wiring or insulation anyway.

Take the cover plates off any electrical switches and receptacles that will be in the way. You will also have to remove light fixtures where ceiling materials must come down, but try to leave them in place as long as possible to use as work lights.

Trim

Remove trim first. If you plan to save it, score along the edge of each piece first with a utility knife. Then pry it off the wall with a flat bar, working gently, and pull the nails out through the back of the piece with a pair of end cutters. Mark or number each piece on the back so you will know later where it goes. You can strip paint off the trim while it is being stored. If you are not saving the trim, simply pry it off and discard.

Removing Floor Coverings

You may be able to install new flooring material directly over the old floor—even a ceramic tile floor—if it is smooth, free of old wax, and securely bonded to the subfloor. Minor cracks, dents, and holes can be patched. It is usually possible to install a new underlayment of plywood or particleboard directly over the present floor if the resulting combination will not be too high. Before you decide to leave the floor covering intact, inspect the subfloor from below for damaged areas that might need repair.

If the subfloor is damaged, if the floor coverings are unstable, or if you wish to expose the wood subfloor and finish it, then you will have to remove the existing floor covering.

Caution: Old resilient flooring may contain asbestos fibers in the backing. They are harmful if inhaled. Cutting, sanding, or breaking the material releases these fibers into the air. Seek professional advice or contact local environmental authorities for recommendations on safely removing asbestos-backed flooring.

Wood

Most wood floors can be repaired and refinished. This is true even of subfloors in good condition. If you wish to remove all or part of a wood floor, the strips can be pried up one by one. Take out the first strip by splitting it with a chisel or cutting out a short section with a circular saw.

Removing Electrical Fixtures

Fixtures and lights can be removed either during the demolition process or when the rough wiring is being installed, depending on how much of the electrical system is being upgraded. Be careful to follow all safety regulations.

Start by turning off the circuit breakers for the kitchen area and put tape over the handles so that no one turns them back on. Cap all hot wires before power is turned back on; double-check all connections before restoring power. If you are removing all the existing lights, you will have to rig up some temporary work lights until your new ones are installed.

Lights

Remove light bulbs, glass globes, or flourescent tubes. Unscrew the mounting nut or nuts and lift the fixture plate away from the wall or ceiling box. Remove any fixture mountings behind the plate. Disconnect the fixture wires from the wires in the box; remove the light fixture; and cap the remaining wires.

If the fixture is heavy, have someone hold it while you disconnect the wires, or temporarily suspend it from the bracket with coat-hanger wire. Save all the fittings if you plan to reuse the fixture.

Switches and Receptacles

Remove the cover plate. With the power off, remove the screws that hold the fixture in place, pull it out, and disconnect the wires. They are either fastened with screws on the side of the switch or receptacle, or inserted into holes in the back and held in place by internal clamps. To release the wire from a clamp, insert a small screwdriver into the appropriate slot. Then cap the wires left in the wall box. Fixtures that are being removed altogether can be left in the electrical box and taken out along with the box and rough wiring.

After demolition, you may still need to do some additional work to prepare for the new installations. This can vary from minor patching and touch-ups to major structural, plumbing, mechanical, electrical, or other work. It is beyond the scope of this book to cover all the techniques that will be involved, but situations unique to kitchens are described below.

Structural Changes

If the project involves adding a room, the shell can be framed and closed in before you open up the wall and disrupt the existing kitchen. However, you will have to take a few extra steps that are not included in simple room additions.

If plumbing, wiring, or any duct work will be run under the floor, it must be installed and inspected before you apply the subflooring over the joists. The exceptions are additions with basements or crawl spaces large enough that a full inspection can be made standing up.

Any plumbing vents, chimneys, flues, or ventilating ducts that penetrate the roof should be installed before the roofing goes on, so that they can be flashed properly.

You may want to leave part of the exterior wall open so that cabinets and debris can be taken out of the

present kitchen and bulky items can be taken in. Once the shell is completed and the present kitchen is gutted, you can proceed as you would with any new construction.

Rough-Framing a Kitchen

The techniques for rough-framing a kitchen are the same as they are for any other room. Start by repairing the floor framing or the subfloor. For the walls and ceiling, there are a few details that occur especially often in kitchens.

Blocking

Wall cabinets are easier to hang if you nail blocking (2 by 10 or 2 by 12) between the studs where the tops of the cabinets will be aligned.

Wing Walls

Short walls (2 to 3 feet long) are often used to enclose a refrigerator, define an alcove, or terminate a row of cabinets. If the walls extend all the way

One of these cabinets is actually a rolling cart. It is used for preparing and serving and doubles as an extra countertop.

from floor to ceiling, frame them like any stud wall and tie the top plates into the ceiling joists or into blocking set between the ceiling joists.

Sometimes, however, a wing wall is designed to reach only part way to the ceiling, creating a feeling of more space and admitting more natural light into an alcove. Because this type of wall has no support along the top or along one entire edge, other means must be used to stabilize it.

If a corner unit, shelf, or counter will be installed against the wing wall and the adjacent wall, it should be enough to brace the wing wall as long as the unit is well secured.

If the wing wall is freestanding, one way to stabilize it is to assemble the framing with screws instead of nails. Another is to stiffen the wall by using thicker wallboard (⅝ inch rather than ½ inch) or plywood. A third method is to anchor the front edge of the wall by using a long 2 by 4 for the last stud, extending it through the floor, and attaching it to a joist or other framing underneath. This is particularly effective for walls that are subject to heavy traffic or that support extensive tile work.

Knee Walls

Also called pony walls, knee walls are low walls that separate the cooking area from the dining, laundry, or other areas, creating an open effect. Frame them the same way as you do full-sized walls, with studs at 16 inches on center, double top plates, and a single soleplate. If one or both ends are freestanding, stabilize the wall as you would a wing wall, adding diagonal or plywood bracing if it has no support at either end. Cover the framing with wallboard.

Pass-throughs

Frame a pass-through the same way as you would a window, with a double rough sill across the bottom and a header to span the top of the opening. If you are cutting into a bearing wall, shore up the ceiling joists on each side of the proposed opening before you cut off any studs. Then, cut the studs off at the height of the pass-through, allowing for the double rough sill and the finish shelf or trim.

Soffits

Soffits consist of a simple "ladder" frame covered with wallboard. It is customary to build them after the wallboard has been installed on the main walls and ceiling. The finished soffit is usually 13 inches wide (even though wall cabinets are only 12 inches wide), to allow for crooked walls or discrepancies in the cabinets. This creates a narrow overhang just above the cabinets, so the wallboard should be covered with a corner bead along this edge.

Use 2 by 2s for framing the soffit to make it easier to drive nails or screws in both directions. Be careful to choose straight lumber, since any warps or bows will show. You can also use 2 by 3s or 2 by 4s, which require toenailing but are more stable.

The easiest method of construction is to build an L-shaped ladder frame on the floor and then secure it in place overhead by nailing or screwing one rail into the ceiling joists and the other into the wall studs.

Windows

When framing windows over a sink or countertop, you will need to decide the height of the finished sill. If the finished sill will be flush with the countertop, be sure to take into account the thickness of any finish flooring material, of the countertop, and of the finished sill, and allow extra clearance for shimming when you lay out the height of the rough sill.

Kitchens are ideal places for garden or greenhouse windows, bay windows, and bow windows. These windows are framed just like any other window. All you need to know is the rough opening dimensions, available from the manufacturer.

Plumbing for a Kitchen

The basic fixtures for most kitchens are a sink, a garbage disposer, and a dishwasher, but your kitchen may also have a bar sink, an ice-making refrigerator, or a washing machine. In addition, a gas line may be needed for the range, cooktop, or oven. If the new fixtures will be installed in the same places as the old ones, just mask the pipes while you work around them. If the new fixtures will be installed within a few inches of the old ones, you may be able to attach pipe extenders to the existing pipes, rather than installing all-new pipes.

Drain and Vent Pipes

In plumbing, the first thing to consider is the drainpipe. A kitchen sink with a dishwasher requires a 2-inch pipe. If you are adding a washing machine to the kitchen drain, most codes require that the pipe be enlarged to 3 inches, all the way to the main drain.

Drainpipes must slope 1/4 inch per foot, so if the existing pipe is strapped

close to the bottom of the floor joists there may not be enough clearance to extend it to the new fixtures. However, if the new pipe can be suspended between the joists there may be enough room for proper slope. If this is not the case, it may be possible to bore holes for a 2-inch drainpipe through the joists, provided they are 2 by 10s or 2 by 12s, and the holes are at least 2 inches from the edges. Otherwise, it will be necessary to hang the new drainpipe below the joists and connect it to the main drain farther downstream in order to get the proper flow.

All plumbing fixtures must be vented to the roof. If the sink is near its original location, use the existing vent. Check your local code for trap-arm distance, the maximum permissible distance between the sink trap and the vent pipe. For a 1½-inch drainpipe, 3 feet is typical; for a 2-inch pipe, up to 5 feet is fine.

Kitchen sinks often have windows over them, making it impossible to run the vent pipe directly up to the roof behind the sink. Codes prohibit changing the direction of the vent pipe from vertical to horizontal at any point lower than 42 inches above the floor, a distance higher than most windowsills. To solve this problem, you can locate the vertical vent pipe to one side of the window and run a horizontal trap-arm from the sink to the pipe (as long as it does not exceed the maximum trap-arm distance permitted by the code). Alternatively, you can offset the vent pipe with two 45-degree fittings to clear the window, thus avoiding a 90-degree change in direction below the 42-inch limit.

Consider the needs of the adjoining room when constructing your new kitchen. A double-fronted cupboard provides access to the good china from the kitchen and the dining room. A pass-through allows dishes to be delivered between the food-preparation countertop and the food-serving buffet.

Water Supply Lines

Run the water supply lines after the drain and vent pipes have been installed. The hot and cold lines for the sink are plumbed like any supply lines. The dishwasher requires a hot-water supply line, usually made of flexible copper tubing, 3/8-inch in diameter, which is connected to an angle stop located under the sink or dishwasher. If the refrigerator has an ice maker, it will need its own cold-water supply line. Check the manufacturer's specifications to determine the size and location of this line. Typically, it is 1/4- or 3/8-inch tubing with a separate angle stop behind or next to the refrigerator.

Rough-in Dimensions

Typical rough-in dimensions for sink pipes are 15 inches above the floor for the drain stub and 19 inches for the hot- and cold-water supply stubs. If the sink is a double-bowl model, you have the choice of centering the drainpipe between the bowls or behind one of the bowls. Consider first on which side you prefer to place the garbage disposer. Your choice also depends on what type of finish connection you will use to tie the two bowls together.

The P-trap for a laundry is usually installed inside the wall behind the washing machine. It must be between 6 and 18 inches off the floor.

Freeze Protection

If you live in a cold climate, take these precautions to keep the water pipes from freezing.
□ Try to run the hot- and cold-water lines within the insulated area, not outside it.
□ Tuck blanket insulation under the drainpipe.
□ Wrap heat tape around any water supply pipes that will be vulnerable to freezing and insulate them.
□ If you use plastic pipe, allow enough slack to provide 6 inches of expansion for every 50 feet of pipe.

Ventilating Ducts

Range hoods should be located 21 to 30 inches above the cooking surface, depending on the capacity of the blower, local code requirements, and the cook's preference.

Plan the duct installation so as to have the shortest possible run with the fewest possible turns. Use uniform size ducts throughout. Maximum length depends on the diameter of the duct and the number of turns—figure 25 feet of straight duct. Turns should not total more than 180 degrees. The duct must terminate outside, not in the attic or crawl space, with an approved roof or wall cap. The termination cap may require a damper, or other means of controlling air movement, and an insect screen. Sheet-metal duct sections of various lengths are available in two shapes—round, for running in free space (attics, closets, crawl spaces), and rectangular, for installing between studs. The manufacturer of the ventilating unit specifies duct size (typically 7 or 8 inches for round ducts and 3 1/4 inches by 10 inches for rectangular ones). Use adjustable rather than rigid elbows for greater flexibility. Various transition pieces are also available; these are used to connect the duct to the fan unit or to join round duct to rectangular duct. Duct materials are readily available from sheet-metal shops or from the dealers who supply the fan units.

Install the duct before you insulate, extending it far enough into the kitchen space so that the remaining pieces can be connected to it when the cabinets and hood are installed. Secure each joint with two sheet-metal screws, drilling pilot holes if necessary. Then seal the joint with metallic or other approved duct tape. If you run a duct between studs and have to cut through the double top plate, reinforce the plate with a metal framing strap.

Wiring for a Kitchen

Wiring is an important part of any kitchen project. Rough wiring consists of installing electrical boxes in the open framing and running the wire or cable to them from the circuit breaker panel or other source. The first step is to plan the circuits. Base the plan on the wiring included with the working drawings and on the provisions of the local code.

Typical Circuit Requirements

You will need a separate circuit for each permanent appliance.
□ Electric range (240 volts)
□ Electric cooktop (240 volts)
□ Electric oven (240 volts)
□ Garbage disposer
□ Dishwasher
□ Microwave
□ In-counter blender motor
□ Trash compactor
□ Freezer

You will also need at least two 20-amp circuits for countertop and other outlets. Outlets in a pantry, breakfast nook, or dining room can be included on these circuits. Codes do not specify how many receptacles to allow for each circuit, but common practice for kitchens is to allow no more than six. It is also customary, where the code permits, to run both circuits together on a three-wire cable. This makes it possible to alternate adjacent receptacles between the circuits, or to split duplex receptacles so that the top half is wired on one circuit and the bottom on the other.

Receptacles over countertops should be located no more than 4 feet apart, with at least one outlet over any section of counter longer than 12 inches. Height is customarily 42 inches above the finish floor.

Lights cannot be connected to any of the circuits described above. Although it may be possible to wire new lights into an existing lighting circuit, there are usually enough lights in a kitchen—especially one that includes a breakfast nook or dining area—to warrant installing a separate 15-amp circuit for them.

Adding New Circuits

There are two things to consider when adding new circuits to the present system: the available space for new circuit breakers (including a double space for each 240-volt breaker) and the electrical capacity of the main service entrance. If the present panel has few or no empty spaces for new breakers, you can either use half-size "wafer" breakers to get more space or install a subpanel (typically 60 amps) for all the new kitchen circuits. Check local codes to find out where the subpanel may be located.

If the present service is properly grounded, if it has a capacity of at least 100 amps, and if you are not adding any major appliances (such as an electric range or dryer) it should be able to handle the new kitchen circuits. Otherwise you may need to upgrade the service entrance.

Installing Electrical Boxes

Following the working drawings, install an electrical box for every switch, light, receptacle, and fixed appliance. Common practice is to center switch boxes 48 inches above the floor, wall outlets 14 inches above the floor, and overcounter outlets 42 inches above the floor. However, you can adjust locations as necessary. For example, you may raise an outlet box to clear a tall back splash behind the counter, or lower a box to conceal it behind a slide-in range.

Note: Most boxes extend out from the studs ½ inch, to accommodate the thickness of standard wallboard. However, sometimes a kitchen outlet must be placed within a back-splash area. In this case, be sure to extend the box far enough beyond the face of the framing to accommodate both the wallboard and the back-splash material. The face of the box must be flush with the finished surface.

Running Electrical Cable

For most installations, codes will allow the use of nonmetallic sheathed cable (Romex™). Use No. 12 cable for all 20-amp circuits and larger sizes for 240-volt circuits. Observe the same rules for running cable in a kitchen as you would in any other room: Staple it every 4½ feet and within 8 inches of plastic boxes and 12 inches of metal boxes. Many local codes do not allow wiring to be run horizontally through exterior wall studs; it must be run under the floor and brought up through the soleplate for each outlet.

Specialty Wiring

Most kitchen wiring is straightforward, but a few points require special attention. One is the matter of smoke alarms. If you are wiring more than one smoke alarm into the house current, link them with three-wire cable (plus ground wire). The extra wire makes it possible to coordinate all the alarms so that all will sound whenever one is activated.

Electrical boxes for some fixtures, such as range hoods, island outlets, and other cabinet outlets, cannot be installed until after the walls are covered and the cabinets are placed. For rough wiring, simply run the cable to the general location of the box and leave a generous length for completing the run when the walls and cabinets are finished.

Although the garbage disposer and dishwasher must have separate circuits, many codes allow them to be wired with a single three-wire cable connected to a duplex receptacle under the sink. Isolate the two halves of the receptacle by breaking the external tab on the hot side and wiring the top half with the black conductor from the three-wire cable and the bottom half with the red conductor. Both halves share the white neutral conductor. At the circuit breaker panel the black and red wires each have their own 20-amp breaker, but the handles must be bonded so that both breakers shut off whenever one is tripped.

Gas Lines

Relocating or adding gas appliances means moving the gas line. This may require increasing the pipe size if the run is very long. You may have to install a larger main gas supply pipe for the entire house. Consult with a plumber about running any new gas lines. You will need to obtain a permit and run a pressure test before completing the installation.

Building Walls and Ceilings

The walls and ceiling of a kitchen are insulated and covered in the same way as other rooms. Apply polyethylene sheeting over the insulation to eliminate potential structural damage from water vapor.

Installing wallboard in the kitchen is a demanding job because of all the cutouts for plumbing, wiring, and duct work. Order a few extra sheets in case you spoil one or two. If you are patching new wallboard into old wallboard or plaster, cut the old material back to a corner, door, or window to make the joint less obvious.

There are several methods for patching holes in existing wallboard. Small holes can be covered with self-sticking fiberglass mesh tape and finished with patching compound. For larger holes, trim the wallboard around the hole to a regular shape, such as a triangle. Cut a patch of wallboard to fit exactly into the hole and a wide strip of plywood or wallboard for backing. Slip the backing inside the wall behind the hole and secure it with wallboard screws or paneling adhesive. Glue or screw the patch to the backing and tape the seams. Patch large holes by cutting the wallboard back to the nearest studs and fitting a new piece.

Most of the baseboard and other trim can be installed at this point. However, do not install the trim that abuts cabinets and built-in appliances until they are in place.

Cabinets are the showpiece of most kitchens. They represent a large share of the cost of renovation as well. Although modular construction makes the work easier, installing cabinets is a meticulous and demanding task. It's easy to underestimate the time required to do it right. For an average-sized kitchen, figure about a week of work for cabinet installation.

In a successful cabinet installation, the units are level, plumb, and square; all joints are tight and flush; and the doors and drawers are aligned. Carefully study the following techniques, along with the manufacturer's instructions, before you start to work. Note especially the differences between frame and frameless cabinet installations. There is no margin for error with frameless cabinets—they must be perfectly square and straight or the doors and drawers will not be square and plumb.

Preparation

Cabinets are installed relatively late in the construction process. All the walls and ceilings should be smooth and—unless you are adding them later—the soffits, if any, should be finished. Painting should be completed, wallcoverings may be up, and wiring for undercounter lighting should be installed. If the finish floor is down, protect it with plywood or cardboard while the cabinets are being installed. Remove paintings and

other valuable objects from the far sides of each wall.

The tools you will need are a ⅜- or ¼-inch electric drill (preferably a variable-speed drill), a countersink bit, an assortment of screwdrivers, a tape measure, a hammer, 2- and 4-foot levels, a 6-foot straightedge or a long level, adjustable clamps or C-clamps, a stepladder, shims, a flat pry bar, masking tape, and a bar of soap. An extra electric drill with a Phillips-screwdriver bit is handy to have. You will also need a supply of 1½-, 2½-, and 3-inch quick-drive wood screws, 3-, 4-, and 6-penny finishing nails, 1-inch brads, and whatever special connecting screws are provided with frameless cabinets.

Inspect all the cabinets for defects and verify the sizes. Make sure that the doors fit, that none of the boxes is

An appliance garage keeps all your small electrical appliances in one place, generally out of sight. The appliances will probably last longer than they would if they were bumped in and out of cupboards and will stay cleaner than they would if they were left out on countertops. Locate the garage near plenty of counter space and easily accessible electrical outlets.

Cabinet Layout

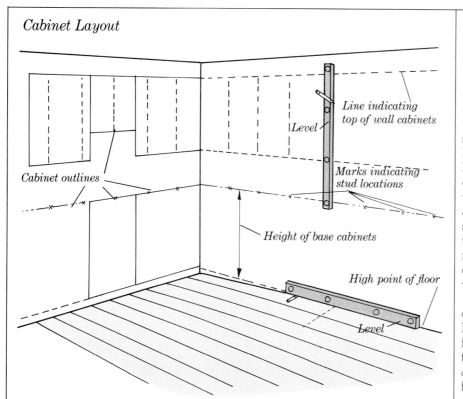

Cabinet outlines

Line indicating top of wall cabinets

Level

Marks indicating stud locations

Height of base cabinets

High point of floor

Level

warped, and that all of the drawers slide perfectly. Remove all of the doors, mark on each door which cabinet it belongs with, and put the cabinets back into the cartons. Store them until you need them.

Start the layout for the cabinets by locating the highest point of the floor in the area where the base cabinets will be installed. Use a long level or a straightedge with a level on it. If the highest point is not against the wall, use a level and a pencil to transfer the height of that point to the wall. Having marked the wall at the appropriate height, measure up from the mark and make a second mark at the height of the base cabinets (usually 34½ inches). Add an allowance for the thickness of the finish floor if it is not yet down and make a third mark. Using the straightedge and a level, draw a line on the wall at this third mark. This line represents the tops of all the base cabinets. (The line will be covered by the counter or the back splash. Make heavy marks on the wall only where they will be covered by cabinets; elsewhere use a faint pencil.)

Now draw another level line for the tops of the wall cabinets. Most wall cabinets are 30 inches tall and 18 inches above the countertop. For most installations, then, this line will be exactly 84 inches (36 + 18 + 30) above the highest point of the floor.

If the wall cabinets extend up to a soffit or up to the ceiling, check them for level. Find the lowest point of the ceiling or soffit in the area over the cabinets and draw a level line on the wall at that height for the cabinet tops. You can now see how much of a gap there will be between the ceiling or soffit and the cabinets. Cover this gap with a strip of molding.

If the installation includes a full-height cabinet, measure it now to make sure that it will fit beneath the ceiling or soffit. You may have to trim the top or the base, according to the manufacturer's instructions.

Using the lines on the wall for horizontal guides and a level for plumb, lay out the cabinet dimensions on the wall. Make sure that they line up properly with each other and

with the various corners, windows, sinks, appliances, and so forth. Make any adjustments necessary.

Next, mark the location of each stud just above the line for the base cabinets, in the area where the upper cabinets will be hung. To find a stud, tap on the wall lightly and listen for a solid sound. Probe the area with a hammer and nail until you locate both edges of the stud. Mark the exact center on the wall. Hold a level vertically against the mark and draw a line for the stud. Repeat for each stud behind the upper cabinets. If there is blocking between the studs, mark another level line at the center of the blocking where the cabinets will be hung.

It is usually easier to install the wall cabinets before the base cabinets. However, if the back splash will be full-height laminate that extends up to the wall cabinets, the base cabinets and the countertop must be installed first. It is also better to install the base cabinets first if there is a full-height cabinet in the middle of a run.

Installing Wall Cabinets

Start a run of wall cabinets with a full-height cabinet or a corner cabinet if you have one. Otherwise start at whichever end will not require a filler piece. The first cabinet is the most critical—it must be perfectly level, plumb, and square, or the entire run will be out of alignment.

Measure where the studs line up behind the first cabinet and transfer these measurements to the inside of the cabinet at the top and bottom hanger rails. Countersink and drill holes through the back of the cabinet at these marks; make the holes just large enough for the 3-inch screws.

If the cabinets are frameless, they may require a metal support rail, provided by the manufacturer. Install this rail next. It must be attached to the wall behind the cabinets, which will be hung from it. Cut it to length and screw it securely to each stud at the height recommended by the manufacturer.

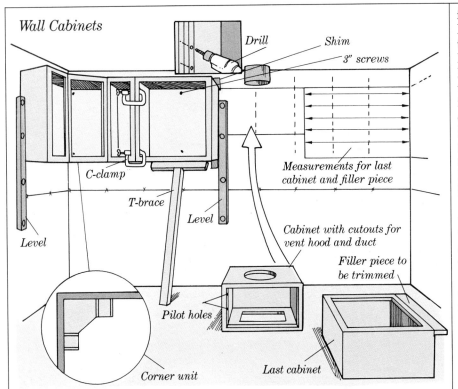

Wall Cabinets

Drill

Shim

3" screws

Measurements for last cabinet and filler piece

C-clamp

T-brace

Level

Level

Cabinet with cutouts for vent hood and duct

Filler piece to be trimmed

Pilot holes

Corner unit

Last cabinet

There are several methods for holding the cabinets in place while you attach them to the wall. One is to build a T-brace slightly longer than the distance between the floor and the bottom of the cabinet. Another method, used when the base cabinets are installed first, is to build a simple rectangular frame out of 2 by 4s; this frame should be just high enough to support the wall cabinets when it sits on a makeshift countertop. A third method can be used if the walls have not yet been finished. Simply screw a 1-by cleat to the wall to support the bottom of the cabinets. Specialty jacks are useful here, if you know a professional who might lend you one.

To begin, lift the first cabinet into place and slide the brace up under it. You will need a helper to stabilize the cabinet while you do this. Screw it to the studs with 3-inch screws, tightening only one of the top screws and leaving the others slightly loose. Place a shim behind the cabinet, next to a screw, at any point where the wall bows inward. Use a level to

check that the cabinet is plumb and horizontal in all directions.

Now transfer the stud dimensions to the inside of the second cabinet and countersink and drill the screw holes. Drill two more screw holes through the vertical stile on the side that will be attached to the first cabinet. Drill where the hinges will cover up the screw heads.

For frameless cabinets the side holes are already partially drilled, about 3 inches back and 2 or 3 inches up from the bottom or down from the top. Simply complete the drilling. Special fasteners go into these holes; they screw into each other, leaving a smooth head on each side that is covered with a plastic cap.

Lift the second cabinet into place and support it, but do not screw it into the back wall. Instead, clamp the two cabinets together so that the joint between them is tight and flush. Use wood shims to protect the cabinet finish from the clamps. Choose a drill bit slightly smaller than the shank of a 1½-inch screw and center it in the

first side hole of the second cabinet. Drill about two-thirds of the way into the adjoining stile of the first cabinet. Do the same for the second side hole. Now lubricate two 1½-inch screws with bar soap and drive them firmly into the holes that you have just drilled. If the cabinets are tall or if the face frames do not align perfectly, predrill more holes and add more screws. Then screw the cabinet to the back wall, the same way as you did the first cabinet.

Repeat this process for all the wall cabinets in the same run. If a vent/hood will be mounted to a wall cabinet, cut holes in the cabinet for the duct before you install it.

If the final cabinet will end next to a sidewall, there may be a gap that needs a filler piece. These come in 3-inch and 6-inch widths and must be cut to fit snugly. Before you install that cabinet, attach the filler piece to the stile in the same way as you would attach two cabinets together. Then take a series of measurements between the wall and the last cabinet installed. Transfer these measurements to the face of the final cabinet, marking them on the filler piece. Now connect the marks with a line. Cut along the line with a fine-toothed keyhole saw, angling the back of the cut toward the cabinet. The cut will follow any deviations in the wall so that the filler piece will fit perfectly. Filler pieces for corners are installed in the same way but need not be scribed and cut. Some manufacturers provide cabinets with wide stiles, called ears, already attached. These ears function as filler pieces and are trimmed in the same way.

When the full run of wall cabinets is in place, check for level, plumb, and squareness (measure diagonals). Use shims to make any necessary adjustments, loosening the back screws to slip them into place. After all the screws are tightened, make a final check. Be especially careful with frameless cabinets. The slightest warp will make the doors hang crooked.

Installing Base Cabinets

Frame and frameless base cabinets are installed in the same way, except that with the frameless style there is no margin for error. Start with a corner cabinet, unless a cabinet in the middle of a run must be perfectly aligned with some other feature, such as a window or the sink plumbing. Set the cabinet in place and shim under the base until the top is even with the layout line. Countersink and drill through the top rail at each stud and attach the rail to the stud with 3-inch screws. If the wall is not straight, place shims behind the cabinet. Use a level to check the top, sides, and front. Hold it against the frame and not against a door or drawer.

Set the second cabinet in place and attach it to the first cabinet, using the same method used for the wall cabinets. Screw it to the back wall.

Complete the run of base cabinets. Some cabinets, such as lazy-Susan corner units and sink fronts, have no box to attach to the wall. They are held in place only at the face frames. (With frameless styles, the sink fronts have sides that extend back just far enough to attach them to the adjacent cabinets.) Because these cabinets have no backs, you will have to provide support for the countertop along the back. Screw cleats of 1-by lumber to the wall just below the layout line.

You will also need to fabricate a floor for some sink fronts. Cut it out of a piece of 1/2- to 3/4-inch plywood and support it on cleats screwed to the wall and the adjacent cabinets. Seal it or paint it before you install it.

If there will be an appliance—a dishwasher, trash compactor, or slide-in range—in the middle of a run, you must allow for it when you install the base cabinets. Check the appliance specifications to determine the exact width of the space. To keep the cabinets on both sides of the gap aligned, bridge the space with a long straightedge at the front and back. Install filler pieces at the end of the run and at the corners, the same way as you did for the wall cabinets.

Finishing Touches

Finish panels, doors, trim, and handles are the most noticeable features of your cabinet installation. Take care to attach them correctly. Try to set aside one day just to do this part of the job; don't try to do it at the end of a long day's work.

In some cabinet lines, finish panels must be installed on all the exposed faces of every cabinet. These panels come either precut or as a full sheet of plywood paneling from which you cut out each piece to fit. If the panels have grain patterns, match each one carefully with the patterns on the adjacent cabinets.

Measure and cut each panel to size. Spread contact cement on the back of each panel and on the side of the cabinet where it goes. Wait for the cement to set, according to the instructions. Press the panel in place, clamp it, and leave it overnight to dry. If necessary, use 3d nails to help hold it in place. The nail heads can be countersunk and the holes filled with putty after the cement dries.

When you put the doors back on the cabinets, some of them may not line up perfectly. Most hinges have a mechanism for making slight adjustments to correct this problem.

Before you install trim pieces, be sure that the cabinets are aligned and securely fastened. Stain or paint the trim; use a miter box to cut it to length, and stain or paint the ends before you attach the trim. Predrill it and fasten it with 3d, 4d, or 6d finishing nails. Sink the heads with a nail set and fill with putty.

For frameless cabinets, attach the trim pieces from inside the cabinet, with screws. Predrill holes through the cabinet large enough to take the screws; use a smaller bit to drill pilot holes in the trim itself. Most manufacturers provide plastic caps to cover the screw heads.

To finish the toe kick, cut baseboard or similar molding to length and paint or stain it a dark color. Attach it to the cabinet kicks with finishing nails.

Installing Shelving

Most cabinet lines include open shelf units to match the cabinets. You can also construct custom-made shelving from hardwood, plywood, or particleboard covered with laminate. You can make a single shelf from an extra filler piece.

Larger units should have adjustable shelves. The simplest and least obtrusive way to build them is to drill a series of holes in the side of the shelf unit into which small brackets can be inserted. These brackets will support the shelves.

There are several ways to harmonize the shelving with the cabinets. You can use the same kind of wood as was used for the cabinets and stain it or paint it to match. Use touch-up stain provided by the cabinet manufacturer. You may want to experiment first with scraps of the same wood. You can also harmonize the shelving with the cabinets by using the same moldings and trim. Finally, you can make the shelf unit the same height as the cabinets and set the shelves at the same heights as the countertop, vent/hood, and other prominent features of the cabinets.

Cabinet Finishes

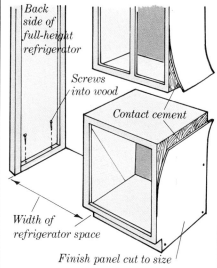

Back side of full-height refrigerator

Screws into wood

Contact cement

Width of refrigerator space

Finish panel cut to size

INSTALLING COUNTERTOPS

*I*nstalling countertops *is exacting but very rewarding work. It involves handling large and fragile pieces of expensive material, taking exact measurements, making precise cuts, producing flawless joints, and attending to minute details. But when it is finished, the large expanse of countertop has a dramatic impact. The kitchen no longer resembles a construction zone. Suddenly the cabinets look finished and beautiful. Your dream kitchen will be a reality in no time.*

Some countertop installations consist simply of laying a slab of material on top of the cabinets and attaching it. Others require joining two or more slabs of material together or fitting the countertop into an awkward space. The most complicated installations involve exotic materials, which must be joined and cut with precision equipment. These installations should be done by professionals. The following techniques cover the installation of plastic laminate countertops, butcher block, marble and granite slabs, solid surface materials, and ceramic tile countertops. In some cases you can do the entire installation yourself; in others, you should hire a professional to fabricate the countertop, which you can then install.

Preparation

The key to a successful installation is careful scheduling, planning, and measuring. Plan ahead. Some materials must be ordered months in advance, and it may take weeks to schedule a professional fabrication or installation. Be sure that the sink, cooktop, and other built-in appliances are on the site at the time the installation is done, or get the manufacturers' specifications for rough-in dimensions. That way you or the installers can make accurate cutouts.

Make as many decisions as possible in advance. Of course, you have already chosen the type of material you will use for the countertops. You must, however, make other decisions about edge details, corners, type and height of back splash, and where to put seams. Try to keep seams away from the sink area in order to prevent water from seeping under the countertop surface.

If you are having countertops fabricated at a shop, do not take final measurements until the walls are finished and the base cabinets are installed. If possible, have the shop take field measurements. If you take your own measurements, make an accurate sketch of the counter area with the dimensions. Keep it handy and make sure to attach a copy to your order so that you and the fabricator can coordinate last-minute changes over the phone.

When measuring, figure a 1-inch overhang in front of the cabinets and at the open ends. Figure a $\frac{1}{8}$-inch overhang where the countertop terminates for an appliance, such as a refrigerator or slide-in range. Where an end butts into a wall that is not square to the back wall, measure the countertop from the longest point. If you are measuring for stock materials that you will cut yourself, such as a butcher block or a postformed laminate top, allow for the thickness of any back-splash and side-splash material that will be attached to the end of the countertop where it abuts a wall. This dimension (which is

usually $\frac{3}{4}$ inch) should be subtracted from the total length of the countertop piece. Make all measurements at least twice.

Finish painting or staining the cabinets before installing the countertops. Make sure that the cabinets have cleats in the corners or along the top edges to which the countertops can be attached. Check the cabinets for level in all directions and build up any low spots by nailing shims to the top edges. If the countertop has a lip it may block the upper drawers, the cutting board, or the dishwasher door. Should this happen, raise the countertop. Nail strips of $\frac{1}{2}$- to $\frac{3}{4}$-inch plywood to the top edges of the cabinet, over the leveling shims, or have the fabricator install padding strips where the countertop will rest on the cabinet.

Installing Laminate Countertops

High-pressure laminate is a thin membrane about $\frac{1}{16}$ inch thick that is bonded to a stable substrate of particleboard or plywood.

You have three options. You can buy the laminate and fabricate your own top; buy sections of ready-made postformed countertop and cut them to size; or order a custom countertop, with or without installation. Postformed countertop is the least expensive and most convenient option—local home centers stock it—but the color selection is limited, the back splash and edge details are fixed, and the sections come in only one width. If you order a custom top, most local shops can obtain nearly any laminate and fabricate a top in any shape. You can save money by installing it yourself, using the techniques described below for postformed tops. You can save more money and customize the work even more by doing the whole job yourself, as long as there are no mitered joints, for which it is virtually impossible to make the proper cuts without specialized equipment.

Installing a Postformed Laminate Countertop

Measure the length of countertop needed, allowing for overhangs and the thickness of any back-splash pieces on the ends. Buy separate end-splash pieces and end caps as needed, as well as drawbolt connectors for any joints. If the countertop is L-shaped, requiring two sections with mitered ends, be sure that each section has the cut at the proper end.

Use a framing square to mark the cut line along the top of the counter and up the back splash. If the corner of the wall is out of square, adjust the cut line to compensate. Place masking tape over the line and draw a fresh line on the masking tape. This protects the edge of the laminate from chipping when it is cut. Make the cut with a sharp crosscut saw that has 10 or 12 teeth to the inch, a saber saw, or a circular saw with a sharp blade. Cut from the back side with a saber or circular saw. Smooth cut edges with a file or plane.

Now attach the end splash, if there is one. This piece is usually a simple rectangle with laminate applied to one side, one long edge, and both short edges. Fit it so that the top edge is flush with the top of the back splash and the front edge is flush with the front of the countertop. Attach it to the end of the countertop with water-resistant glue and screws. Predrill pilot holes for the screws.

If there is no side splash, cover the exposed end of the countertop with a special end cap. To support the bottom and back edges of the end cap, glue or screw ½-inch by ½-inch wood strips to the bottom and back of the countertop, flush with the end. Then sand the wood surfaces smooth and glue the end cap in place with contact cement. Seal the bottom of the countertop with primer.

Set the countertop in place, snug against the back wall and the side-wall. If gaps appear due to irregularities in the wall, you need to do a little custom fitting. By sliding a pencil along the wall, scribe a line along the top edge of the back splash that is

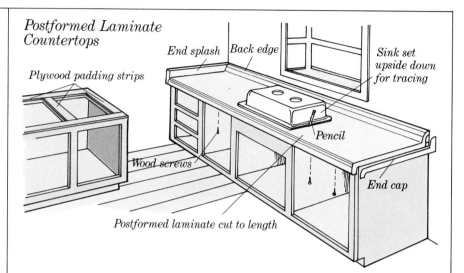

Postformed Laminate Countertops

Plywood padding strips · *End splash* · *Back edge* · *Sink set upside down for tracing* · *Wood screws* · *Pencil* · *End cap* · *Postformed laminate cut to length*

parallel to the back wall. Then pull the countertop out from the wall and trim away any excess on the backside of the line with a file, block plane, or belt sander. For L- or U-shaped countertops, set both sections in place and fit them snugly together before scribing them.

Next, lay out the openings for the sink, the cooktop, and the drop-in range. A sink cutout should start 1¾ inches back from the front edge. Mark a line at this point. This will be the front line. Now find the centerline of the sink by measuring from the sidewall to the center of the sink cabinet. Transfer this line to the countertop. Allow for any overhangs. If the sink has its own rim, set it upside down on the countertop. Center it over the centerline and pull the front edge of the sink about ½ inch forward of the front line. Trace around it. Then remove the sink and draw the cut line about ½ inch inside the tracing. This ½-inch allowance should be adequate to support the rim and still clear the bowl. Check your measurements again. Make sure that the bowl of the sink will clear the cabinets, too. Some sink manufacturers include a paper template for tracing. Rimless sinks require a separate rim, usually of stainless steel. Set this rim on the countertop and trace around it in the same way as you would for a rimmed sink.

You can cut out the opening now or after the countertop is installed. Drill a ¾-inch hole inside the cut line at each corner to start the saber saw. When you reach the back splash, there may not be enough room for you to use a saber saw. Cut from the bottom of the countertop or use a keyhole saw. Avoid making square corners on cutouts; they tend to start cracks. Drill holes at each corner or round the corners with a saber saw.

For L- and U-shaped countertops, assemble the sections before you attach them to the cabinets. After checking the fit, slide the pieces slightly forward so that there is room to separate them and move them around. Make sure that you have access to the bottom of the joint. If necessary, set the pieces upside down, in position, on padded saw-horses or a makeshift workbench.

Apply waterproof glue or silicone sealant to the edges to be joined and slide the pieces together. Align them carefully. Install the drawbolts in the recessed cavities and tighten them with an open-end wrench. Feel along the top of the joint as you tighten them to be sure that the two surfaces are absolutely flush.

Fasten the countertop to the cabinets from below with screws that are long enough to penetrate the countertop ½ inch. Apply a thin bead of caulk between the countertop and the wall.

Fabricating a Laminate Countertop On-site

Use ¾-inch high-density particle-board (minimum 45-pound grade) or dense plywood for the substrate. Cut all countertop and back-splash pieces to exact size. Glue and screw ¾- by ¾-inch strips beneath the front and side edges of the countertop for the overhang. The base should be clean, smooth, and dry, and joints in the base should not coincide with joints in the laminate.

Cut the laminate to size, allowing an extra ¼ inch along any edges that can be trimmed. Mark the cutting lines with a knife blade. Cut with a specialty tool called a laminate cutter or use a saw with a fine-toothed blade. Cut the laminate facedown if you use a saber saw or circular saw, and faceup if you use a handsaw or a table saw. If you use a table saw for cutting narrow strips, clamp a piece of wood onto the fence just high enough above the table to keep the laminate from chattering as it passes through the blade.

If two pieces will be joined, overlap the ends and cut both pieces at the same time with a router. Guide the router with straightedges clamped along both sides. Use a straight carbide cutting bit.

Attach the edge strips first. Apply contact cement to both surfaces. When the cement is dry to the touch, bond the laminate to the substrate, being careful to position it perfectly before the surfaces make contact. Go over the laminate with a roller or with a hammer and padded wood block to ensure a good bond. For rounded edges, soften the laminate with a flameless heater, such as a hair dryer, and then bend it. Use a router with a straight carbide flush bit to trim the edges. File the top edge so that it is flush with the substrate.

To attach the top piece, spread contact cement on both surfaces with a paint roller (unlike most adhesives, contact cement only sticks to itself). While it is drying, lay clean sticks on the substrate to keep the laminate from making contact as you position it. Lay the laminate on the sticks and align it. Then, working from the center, slide the sticks out from under the laminate and press it down into place. Trim the edges with a router, using a carbide bevel cutter with a ball bearing tip, to produce a beveled edge.

Install the countertop the same way as you would a postformed unit. If you use wood trim for the edges instead of laminate, attach the top first and trim it as you would an edge strip. The wood edging should be stained and sealed, or painted, ahead of time. Seal the exposed edge of the substrate as well. Attach the wood strip with glue and finishing nails.

Countertops are a key visual feature of any kitchen, and special care must be given to the selection of the surface treatment. Here, a solid surface–material countertop is trimmed with wood stained to match the cabinet trim, tying the two elements into a cohesive design. The drawers under the cooktop can accommodate oversized cooking pots.

Installing Butcher-Block Countertops

Made from hardwoods, such as sugar maple, red oak, and white ash, butcher-block countertops are available in 25-inch widths and in various lengths. Most blocks are 1½ inches thick. They can form an entire countertop or a section of one.

Measure for butcher block the same way as you would for any countertop and cut the block to exact length. Cut from the top with a handsaw or from the bottom with a circular power saw, using a straightedge. Paint the cut end immediately with a urethane or lacquer sealer to prevent splitting.

If the back edge will not be covered by back-splash material, set the block in place, check for irregularities in the back wall or sidewalls, and trim the block to fit. Seal the raw wood.

Before the final installation, drill holes through the cabinet cleats to take the mounting screws. Changes in humidity cause the wood block to expand and contract in width (although not in length). To allow for these fluctuations, use a bit at least ⅜-inch larger than the diameter of the screws. This will permit the mounting screws to move with the block.
Set the countertop in place and secure it with screws or lag screws long enough to penetrate 1 inch into the block. Predrill to avoid splitting, using a bit smaller than the diameter of the threads. Use a washer to hold the screw against the cabinet cleat and tighten the screw only enough to make contact. Set a screw in each corner of the block.

You can detail the edges and the corners of a butcher-block countertop in various ways: Trim the corners by sawing off the tips; round the edges with a router; put a bevel or an ogee on the edges with a router; or round the corners with a saber saw. After cutting, sand the raw surfaces smooth and seal them with a satin urethane finish.

Installing Natural-Stone Slab Countertops

Natural marble has been used on counters and tabletops for centuries, and other natural stones, such as slate and granite, are becoming popular. A slab is heavy and difficult to cut; have a simple slab cut to size and edged by the supplier. You can then install it yourself. Leave large or complicated installations to the professionals. Be sure to tell the dealer not to leave sharp corners on countertops for islands and peninsulas. They are dangerous, especially if the household includes toddlers.

Measure carefully for the top and the back splash. If the marble section will be lower than the adjacent countertops (if you are installing a marble confectioner's slab, for example), allow for side pieces where the counter returns to the standard height. These side pieces can be made of matching stone or any other appropriate material. Take the measurements to a marble dealer and have the pieces cut and edged.

Position the counter, back, and the end pieces to make sure that they are even with the other counter surfaces and back splashes. If they are too low, nail plywood shims to the top of the cabinet frame to bring them up.

Apply an adhesive recommended by the supplier to the top of the cabinet frame and set the counter slab in place. Use the same adhesive to attach the back splash to the stone top and to the back wall. Follow this procedure for the end pieces as well.

Run a bead of silicone sealant along all the seams and points of contact with the back wall and the adjacent counters. Shape and smooth the bead with a damp rag wrapped around your finger.

Finish the countertop with sealer, using whichever product the supplier recommends. Apply it according to the instructions on the label.

Installing Solid Surface-Material Countertops

Large countertops or complicated installations with laminated edges, joints, and inlays should be left to the professionals. A simple slab, however, is fairly easy to install.

Sheets in ½- and ¾-inch thicknesses are used for countertops. Countertops can have sinks molded into them. Special 5-inch-wide strips are available for back splashes.

Start by measuring the length and width of the countertop area. Allow about 1 inch for each overhang. Install a ¾-inch plywood base over the cabinets to mount the countertop on. Shim, if necessary, to make it level. For a recessed sink, cut out the opening and then rout a groove around the edge so that the sink rim rests flush with the top of the plywood. Provide extra support for the sink by attaching cleats under the edges of the opening.

Cut the countertop and the back splashes to size. Use a circular power saw with a carbide-tipped blade and cut from the backside of the slab, or according to manufacturers' instructions. Wear goggles. Clamp a straightedge to the countertop to guide the saw. (Protect the finished surface with masking tape.) For sink openings, cut the straight lines with a circular saw and the corners with a saber saw. Set the top in place to check for fit.

To create a thicker edge, turn the top over and attach pieces of trim along the edge, using an adhesive recommended by the manufacturer. Clamp the joints and let them dry overnight. You can do the same for the back splash, or you can attach it after the top is in place.

Fasten the countertop to the plywood base or to the cabinet tops, using a mastic recommended by the manufacturer. Attach the back splash and seal all joints with silicone. Wipe away the excess and smooth the sealant with a damp rag.

Installing Ceramic Tile Countertops

Tile is an excellent do-it-yourself material for countertops and back splashes. It is especially suitable for tops that have many corners, angles, and complicated shapes. It can be installed directly over an old laminate countertop, as long as the latter is in good condition. Ask a tile dealer to recommend the best adhesive for this particular job. Tile installation is relatively inexpensive, although special trim pieces and epoxy adhesives can drive the cost up quickly.

Unglazed tiles are not appropriate for countertops. They stain easily and they absorb moisture. Always use glazed ceramic tiles for countertops—especially around sinks and as food preparation surfaces.

Purchase tiles that are rated for use on horizontal surfaces. These tiles are thicker than the ones that are manufactured for use on walls. If they are made of ceramic, they will usually be ½ inch thick. Polished dimensioned-stone tiles ⅜ inch thick can be used for countertops as well.

Choose the trim and accent pieces early and buy them with the tile. Trim tiles are not always available to match every tile pattern, so you may have to choose a different pattern if you need to buy trim.

Installing tile countertops always involves these same basic steps: Prepare the backing, perform a dry tile layout, draw the working lines, apply the adhesive, set the full tiles, set the cut tiles, grout, caulk, and seal. All but the first two of these steps are the same as those for installing ceramic tile on floors (see page 102). Both jobs also require the same tools.

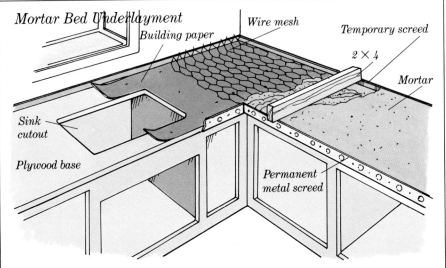

Mortar Bed Underlayment
Building paper
Wire mesh
Temporary screed
2 × 4
Mortar
Sink cutout
Plywood base
Permanent metal screed

Tile Backings

Start by installing a ⅝- or ¾-inch plywood substrate over the base cabinets. The best installations are done on a bed of mortar ¾ inch to 1 inch thick, but an acceptable installation for kitchen counters would be ½-inch Glass Mesh Mortar Unit (GMMU) nailed to a ¾-inch plywood base. GMMU is a cement and fiberglass board designed as a backing for tile installations; it is especially suited for use in wet areas. It can also be used as a backing for the back splash.

Cut GMMU sheets by scoring and snapping, using a utility knife or a saw. Work on the coated side of the unit. Precut each unit and make any necessary cutouts prior to installation. Position the GMMU over the plywood with the coated side up. Secure each unit with 1½-inch galvanized or rust-resistant nails or 1¼-inch galvanized coarse-thread sharp-point screws. Drive the fasteners flush with the coated surface but do not countersink them.

To prevent any leakage through the GMMU, apply 2-inch glass mesh tape over all joints and around all cutouts. Cover the tape with the setting adhesive. For best results allow these joints to dry before you begin to install the tiles.

Tile can also be attached directly to a plywood backing, but this method requires sealing the plywood carefully, using epoxy-based mastic, and adding latex or epoxy modifiers to the grout mix.

If you are not adding a mortar float or GMMU to the top, raise the plywood by attaching 1 by 3 strips to the bottom along the edges. This provides a backing for the tiles along the front edge and keeps them from interfering with the drawers. Screw the top in from below to make future removal easier. Use shims if necessary to make it level.

Cut out openings for the sink and the surface appliances (see page 89). If you are installing a recessed sink, set it in place now. Surface-mounted sinks are installed after tiling.

To install a mortar float, nail a special metal screed strip around the outer edges of the countertop with the top edge extending 1 inch above the plywood substrate. Measure and cut a piece of building paper to cover the plywood. Cut reinforcing wire mesh to size, lay it over the paper, and staple it to the plywood. Mix mortar to a consistency dry enough that it will stick in a ball and not ooze water. Lay a strip of wood lath 1 inch high against the back wall. Spread the mortar over the countertop and screed it level by dragging a straight-edge along the tops of the screed strips. Let it set up for an hour or two before setting tile.

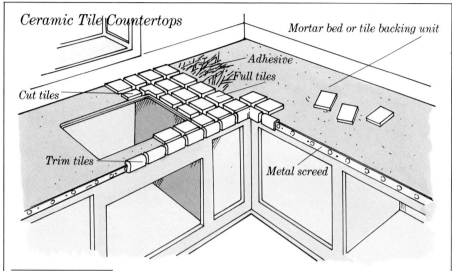

Ceramic Tile Countertops

Cut tiles
Trim tiles
Adhesive
Full tiles
Mortar bed or tile backing unit
Metal screed

Dry Tile Layout

Dry tile layout is the act of completely designing the tile installation before a single tile is stuck in place. It allows you to position tiles in their exact location so that you use as many full tiles and as few cut tiles as possible. A dry tile layout is practical only for small installations, such as countertops.

First, tape any trim tiles along the edge; then start taping the field tiles. If the counter is L-shaped, start the layout at the inside corner and work outward. The inside corner piece should be a full tile. For straight counters, start with full tiles at the front and work toward the back. On islands and peninsulas without sinks or other inserts, begin setting full tiles at the measured center point of the field and work out toward the trim in all directions. Use tile spacers to maintain uniform grout lines. All of the trim pieces should be laid out so that the grout lines match up with the grout lines of the field tiles.

Because they tend to be less stable, avoid setting very small cut tiles at the counter back and around the sink and other inserts. If the sink is surface mounted, mark tiles for cutting by laying them in place and scribing them from beneath. Cut them with

a tile cutter or nippers. The sink rim will cover the raw edges. If the sink is recessed, fit the trim pieces around it and cut the field tiles where they abut the trim pieces, allowing for the grout line. These cuts must be smooth and accurate because they will not be covered by a sink rim, so it is best to make them as you are setting the tile.

Once you are satisfied with the design, mark working lines on the setting bed so that you can reproduce it when you install the tiles. For a countertop with a sink or range insert, mark working lines around the cutout to position the trim tiles around the fixture. Extend the countertop working lines up the back splash to keep the tiles aligned.

Installing Tiles

Spread the adhesive and set the tiles exactly as if you were installing floor tiles (see page 102). When you have finished the last row of countertop tiles, work up the back-splash wall. Use bullnose tiles along the top edge. When you have finished, remove the excess adhesive from the tiles as quickly as possible. Then let the work dry for one or two days. You may need to tape the back splash and trim tiles in place while the adhesive dries.

After about 24 hours, grout the joints, as described on page 103. Then cover the countertop with plastic sheeting for two or three days to let the grout cure properly.

Special Situations

Most countertops are installed directly over base cabinets at a standard 36-inch height, but there are exceptions. Sometimes, for example, you may want to change the height of the countertop. If a tall cook prefers a higher countertop, raise the cabinets by building a simple platform of 1-by or 2-by lumber to set them on. Many cooks, on the other hand, prefer a lower countertop for baking, or wheelchair access, or to match the height of a standard 30-inch table. Base cabinets are almost always 34½ inches high, but you can use 24-, 27-, or 30-inch wall cabinets and install them on a platform set back slightly to provide a toe kick. Typically, wall cabinets are only 12 inches deep, while base cabinets are 24 inches deep, so either set them 12 inches out from the wall or install a narrow countertop.

Countertops that are not adequately supported by cabinets require other structural support. Examples are a sideboard mounted on a wall, or a peninsula countertop that extends beyond the cabinets so that stools or chairs can be pulled up beneath it. For a countertop, such as a sideboard, that is wholly unsupported by cabinets, set the back or the ends on wall cleats and use diagonal braces. For a countertop that extends beyond the cabinets, you can support a wide overhang by using 1-inch or 1¼-inch plywood as the base. This distance is limited for fragile countertop materials like tile. This works best with plastic laminates, which can be used this way for very wide extensions.

Some kitchen countertops are not intended for food preparation or eating. Examples are desktops and laundry counters. Use appropriate materials for these countertops and the same installation techniques described above.

INSTALLING SINKS AND FAUCETS

Sinks come in many styles. They are made of enameled cast iron, stainless steel, enameled steel, porcelain, synthetic marble, and lightweight composite materials. Plus, they come in single-bowl, double-bowl, and other configurations.

Some sinks will accommodate various special fixtures. Besides the faucet, you may want to install a sprayer, a dishwasher air gap, an instant hot-water dispenser, a soap dispenser, or some other accessory on the sink deck. In spite of all these options, installation techniques are essentially the same for all sinks; the only real difference is in how they are mounted to the countertop.

Recessed sinks are mounted into the base before the countertop material is installed. This material may extend slightly over the rim of the sink or butt up to it for a flush surface. Surface-mounted sinks are either self-rimming, or have a separate metal rim that creates a low profile. Both types are mounted after the countertop material is installed.

Most recessed sinks are cast iron, porcelain, or double-wall stainless steel. Many sinks made of thinner materials tend to expand and contract too much to be appropriate for this type of installation.

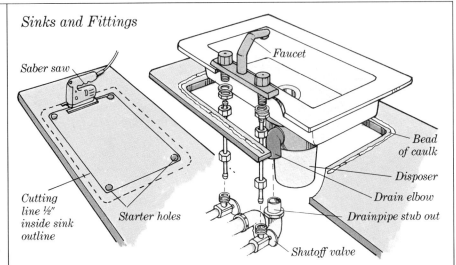

Sinks and Fittings

Saber saw

Cutting line ½" inside sink outline

Starter holes

Faucet

Bead of caulk

Disposer

Drain elbow

Drainpipe stub out

Shutoff valve

Sink Installation

Sinks are installed as follows: Mark and cut the opening as described for laminate countertops, page 89. The front edge of the opening should be at least 1¾ inches from the edge of the counter. Leave more space if the countertop is wider than 25 inches, but do not leave more than 3 to 4 inches of space.

In some cases the cabinet may interfere with sink clearances below the cutout. If it does, cut enough of the cabinet for proper clearance.

For suface-mounted sinks with a separate metal rim, attach the rim to the sink before installing it. Apply a thin bead of caulk around the top of the sink rim, slide the rim over it, and punch in the tabs on the side of the rim to lock it onto the sink. Wipe off the excess caulk.

Attach the faucet, drain, and other accessories to the sink before you install it. Support the sink on sawhorses for easier access to the top and bottom. Apply plumber's putty around the drain hole before you install the strainer assembly or garbage disposer drain. Use large slip-joint pliers to tighten the lock nut from below.

Plan which holes on the sink deck you want to use for various fixtures. If there are not enough predrilled holes, you can install the dishwasher air gap directly in the countertop instead of in the sink to free one of the holes for some other fixture.

Most faucets include flexible copper supply tubes. Insert the tubes through the sink hole while they are slightly curved (slip the sealing gaskets over them first). Be careful not to kink the tubing when you bend it. With the faucet in place, attach the

mounting nuts and washers from below. Use a basin wrench to reach into tight spaces. Attach the sprayer according to the instructions provided by the manufacturer.

Attach the rest of the fixtures following the manufacturer's instructions. Instant hot-water dispensers require a cold-water hookup. Install either a three-way angle stop to the cold-water stub, or plumb in an extra cold-water angle stop under the sink. Then run flexible copper tubing from the angle stop to the dispenser. Also, provide an electrical outlet under the sink, separate from the dishwasher and the garbage disposer.

Apply a bead of silicone caulk around the edge of the sink opening and set the sink in place. You will need help to lift a cast-iron sink. Sinks with metal rims, stainless steel sinks, and lightweight composite sinks have mounting clips, which you install from below and tighten with a screwdriver. Space them about 8 inches apart and near each corner.

Connect the water supply inlets to the shutoff valves with water supply tubing. Install the garbage disposer, the drain arms, and the P-trap. Before you turn the running water back on, remove the aerator attachment from the end of the faucet spout and leave if off for a few days. There may be debris in the pipes left over from roughing-in the plumbing.

INSTALLING LIGHT FIXTURES

*I*nstalling new kitchen light fixtures is a job that can be handled easily by even a novice do-it-yourselfer. General guidelines are presented here. However, the precise mounting methods vary with the individual model. Always refer to the manufacturer's instructions.

Before you begin to install the light fixtures, make sure that the electrical boxes are in place. If the fixture weighs more than 5 pounds, the box should be attached directly to a joist or a bar hanger. The circuit wiring should be properly grounded; make sure that the ground wire in each box is attached directly to the grounding screw. If there are several cables coming into the box, all the ground wires should be joined together, and a short pigtail wire should be run between them and the grounding screw. Wires from the switches should be designated black; neutral wires are white. Be sure to turn off the power to the electrical boxes before you start to install the fixtures.

Installing Pendant and Surface-Mounted Fixtures

Fixtures mounted to the ceiling surface or suspended on rods or chains all have a canopy or housing that is attached to the electrical box with screws or a central threaded stud. Generally, heavy fixtures—those weighing over 30 pounds—must be supported by a threaded stud mounted inside the box.

Prepare the electrical box by attaching whatever stud or bracket is

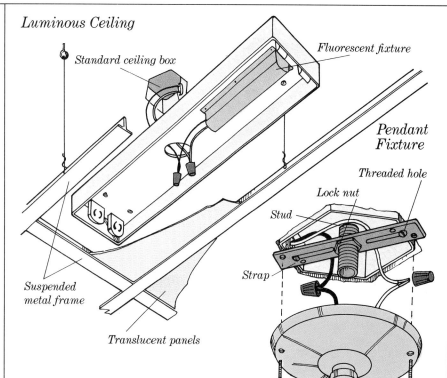

Luminous Ceiling

Standard ceiling box

Fluorescent fixture

Pendant Fixture

Threaded hole

Lock nut

Stud

Strap

Suspended metal frame

Translucent panels

required. For screw-mounted fixtures, make sure that the holes in the fixture canopy line up with the threaded holes at the edge of the electrical box, or use a mounting strap.

Use wire nuts to attach the fixture wires to the house wires. If the fixture is heavy, have a helper hold it; if you are working alone, hang it from the electrical box with coat hanger wire while you make the connections.

Secure the fixture canopy to the ceiling with the two finish screws provided or with a decorative nut for the threaded stud. Install the light bulb, turn on the power, and verify that the light is functioning before you add the finish pieces.

Installing a Luminous Ceiling

A ceiling or partial ceiling of translucent panels consists of fluorescent fixtures attached to the ceiling and a

separate set of translucent panels mounted beneath them. The panels are either suspended from the ceiling on a metal grid or mounted flush into a false ceiling built slightly below the main ceiling. They can also be installed flush with the main ceiling if a recessed cavity is built into the attic to house the fluorescent fixtures. The light fixtures can be installed before or after the grid is in place.

Mount each fluorescent fixture to the ceiling beneath an electrical box, threading the house wires through a knockout hole in the top of the fixture. Attach the fixture to the ceiling with wood screws driven into ceiling joists or toggle bolts inserted through holes in the ceiling surface. Secure the house wires with a clamp and connect them to the fixture wires with wire nuts. Install the fluorescent tubes and turn on the power.

Set the translucent panels into the grid spaces, twisting them slightly to get them up through the grid.

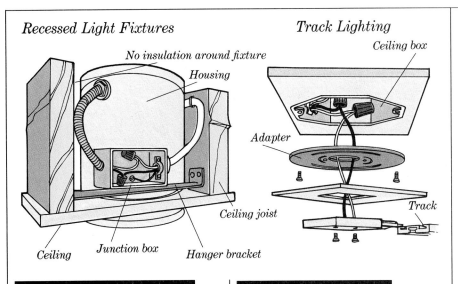

Recessed Light Fixtures

No insulation around fixture

Housing

Ceiling

Junction box

Hanger bracket

Ceiling joist

Track Lighting

Ceiling box

Adapter

Track

Installing Translucent-Panel Fixtures

Fluorescent fixtures with one or two translucent panels come in self-contained units that are either recessed into the ceiling or mounted on the surface. Surface-mounted units are installed directly beneath an electrical box, and the house wiring in the box is threaded through a knockout hole in the top of the housing. The housing and wiring are connected in the same way as they would be for a standard fluorescent fixture.

A recessed fixture requires a large cutout in the ceiling. Joists or blocking should frame the opening above the surface material. Some fixtures are small enough to fit between the ceiling joists. Others are too wide; for these you must cut out a section of a joist. Support the cut ends with headers nailed between adjacent joists. Run Romex nonmetallic cable or similar approved wiring to the general area of the opening. Thread it through a knockout hole in the fixture box as you lift the fixture housing into place. Secure the housing to the framing with screws or nails. Make the wiring connections inside the housing. Install the fluorescent tubes, test the light, and set the translucent panels in place.

Installing Recessed Fixtures

The metal housing for most recessed fixtures is installed before the wallboard goes on the ceiling, so at this point you need only install the trim ring and the light bulb. Be sure that the housing is installed according to the manufacturer's instructions and follow any specified precautions concerning insulation and clearances.

Because the finish trim and the hardware are installed so much later than the housing, they can easily be misplaced or damaged in the interim. Mark the cartons well and store them in a safe place.

There are various methods of installing trim rings. Most models have a spring device on each side that hooks onto tabs located inside the metal housing. Use needle-nose pliers to make installation easier.

Special cut-in fixtures are available that can be installed in an existing ceiling. Cut a hole in the ceiling just large enough for the housing to pass through, or as specified by the manufacturer. This serves as an access hole to do the wiring above the ceiling. Fish Romex nonmetallic cable up to the hole from the light switch. Most fixtures include a junction box, which is connected to the housing with flexible armored cable. Pass the junction box up through the hole, with the

fixture dangling below it, and attach it to the nearest rafter. Fish the non-metallic cable into the junction box and make the electrical connections. Push the fixture housing up into the hole and tighten the securing clamps from inside the housing. Attach the trim ring the same way as you would for a rough-in housing.

Installing Track Lights

The tracks are mounted to a canopy plate that fits over a standard electrical box. Use the old light fixture box or install a new box. It can be wired so that the switch or switches operate all the track lights at once, or so that two separate switching circuits each operate only certain lights. The plate can be located at the end of the track, in the middle, or at the intersection of a T. For each location there is an appropriate attachment.

Mount the canopy bracket supplied with the track on the ceiling electrical box. It is grooved or slotted to accept the track and wire connector. If the holes in the bracket don't match up with the holes in the electrical box, use an adapter ring that offers several adjustable combinations of holes. Connect the wires of the track connector to the house wires with wire nuts and screw the canopy bracket to the electrical box or the adapter ring.

The track is held to the ceiling or wall with mounting clips aligned with holes in the track. Use the track or a straightedge to mark on the ceiling the points where the mounting clips should be located. Attach them with screws or toggle bolts, predrilling first. Snap the track into the wire connector and the mounting clips.

Snap the light fixtures into the track and secure them with the locking levers or similar devices provided by the manufacturer. Turn on the power and adjust the lights to achieve the best effect. Slide them closer together or farther apart as necessary, and then relock the levers.

Installing a Garden Window

Garden or greenhouse windows fit into a standard window opening. Obtain the rough-in dimensions of the unit before you frame in the opening. Most units have metal mounting flanges around the outside, which are attached to the exterior sheathing or framing. If you are installing a garden window in an existing window opening, you may have to modify that opening by enlarging it or by filling part of it in. It is relatively easy to enlarge an opening by lowering the sill, but to widen or raise an opening you will have to alter the main header. This involves substantial structural changes.

If the outside wall around the opening is covered with siding, remove enough to attach the mounting flanges to the sheathing or framing. Trim the opening with paper flashing first. Apply a liberal bead of caulk around the opening and set the window in place. Tuck the top mounting flange under the paper flashing and secure one corner with a 1½-inch roofing nail. Then adjust the unit so that it is level and plumb and finish nailing the flange.

Cover the mounting flange with new siding or with pieces of 1-by trim. Finish the inside of the framed window opening with wallboard butted to the metal window frame or with a wood jamb.

Installing a Skylight

The rafter and ceiling alterations for the skylight should be done when you do the rest of the rough framing, and the skylight itself should be installed before the wallboard goes up. You will need sheet-metal step flashing, custom-fabricated top and bottom curb flashings, and extra roofing shingles. If a curb is not included, build one out of 2 by 6s. The outside dimensions of the curb should be ¾ inch less than the inside dimensions of the skylight frame.

Lay out the rough opening on the roof by driving a nail up from below at each corner of the skylight frame. The dimensions of the opening should equal the inside dimensions of the skylight curb. Remove a section of roofing approximately 6 inches wider all around than the dimensions of the rough opening. Then cut out the opening.

Toenail the curb into the roof sheathing, making sure that it is square and not torqued. Set the skylight over the curb to test the fit. There should be about ⅜ inch of clearance all around. The inside of the curb should be flush with the edges of the roof opening.

Patch in the new roofing shingles, using the custom-fabricated curb flashings and step flashing around the curb. Nail the step flashing into the side of the curb, not into the roof deck. Apply caulk or weather stripping around the top edge of the curb and set the skylight down over it. Secure skylight with special aluminum twist nails that have neoprene gaskets. Nail them through the side of the skylight frame into the curb.

Because the window over the stove looked out on the alley where the garbage cans are stored, these homeowners decided to turn their view indoors. This stained-glass scene is a modified bay window.

INSTALLING FLOORING

*T*he timing of the flooring installation depends on the material involved and on the extent of your remodeling plans. Most floor coverings can be installed either before or after the base cabinets are in place. If you are not replacing the base cabinets, install the flooring toward the end of construction, after painting, to minimize damage to the new floor.

Wood, noncoved resilient sheet flooring and tile, and ceramic and dimensioned-stone tile are easier to install before the base cabinets are in place, because less measuring and cutting is involved. Full pieces can be laid down where the ends will be covered by the cabinets. There is also more working space available for the installer. If the flooring has a border design or a strong pattern, it should be installed with the location of the cabinets in mind, no matter when the installation is done. Installing the flooring before the cabinets requires more material, which could be a consideration with expensive flooring. Uneven materials, such as slate or handmade tile, should be installed after the cabinets are in place. Carpet is always installed last.

The key to a good installation is preparation of the subfloor and the framing. Begin by inspecting them for rot damage, structural weaknesses, and surface deformities. If you are removing the old flooring you can inspect the subfloor from above, but any structural damage to the framing may go unnoticed unless you also inspect from below. Pay close attention to the sink area, even

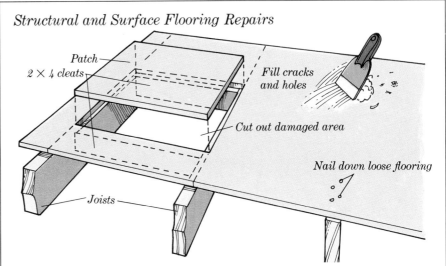

Structural and Surface Flooring Repairs

Patch

2 × 4 cleats

Fill cracks and holes

Cut out damaged area

Nail down loose flooring

Joists

if it means making inspection holes in a downstairs ceiling. If you find damage, repair it at this time, whether the new flooring is installed now or later.

Structural Repairs

Rotted or badly damaged subflooring should be replaced. Cut out a rectangular section of subfloor around the damaged area. The cutout should extend at least 12 inches beyond any rotted wood and the edges should be centered over floor joists. Use a circular saw with the blade set to the depth of the subflooring, so that you don't cut any joists. Cut a replacement patch out of plywood of the same thickness as the subfloor, allowing 1/16 inch to 1/8 inch of clearance around it for expansion. Nail 2 by 4 blocking between the joists to support the edges of the patch. Set the patch in place and nail it to the joists and the blocking with wallboard nails.

Extensive structural repair will require professional help. If the damage is limited to one or two floor joists, simply nail a length of 2-by lumber of the same thickness next to the damaged joist. Nail along the top edge, bottom edge, and center with 12-penny (12d) or 16d common nails. If the damage is due to rot,

support the joist on both sides of the rotted section with temporary shoring and cut the section out. Then splice a new joist to the truncated joist. Make it long enough to rest on the girders or other bearing members, or at least long enough to extend beyond the empty section 4 feet or more in each direction. Fasten the two joists together with 12d or 16d common nails.

Surface Repairs

If the subfloor is sound, it is not necessary to take up the existing floor in order to install a new one. If the new materials are compatible with the old ones, simply remove all dirt, grease, and wax from the existing flooring; patch any holes or other damage; and install the new floor.

However, if the new materials are not compatible with the old ones, you must first cover the existing floor with a suitable backing. Different types of flooring require different types of backing. For resilient flooring, 5/16-inch particleboard or 1/4-inch plywood (plugged and touch sanded) will do. If you are installing ceramic or dimensioned-stone tiles use glass mesh mortar units. GMMU is not a structural underlayment, but it does provide waterproofing protection and it is an excellent backing for a tile installation.

Installing Resilient Sheet Flooring

Thin sheet materials must be installed over a perfectly smooth surface. Otherwise, nail holes, cracks between the boards, and even specks of sawdust will show through. Furthermore, the backing must be moistureproof. Try to find a roll wide enough that it will not require a seam. Rolls usually come in 6-foot or 12-foot widths, but 15-foot widths are sometimes available. If seams are necessary, plan them for the narrowest part of the kitchen or away from highly visible, heavy-traffic areas. Choosing a pattern with straight lines also helps to conceal any seams.

There are three options for attaching resilient sheet: loose laying, with only a few staples around the edges; gluing just the perimeter; and gluing the full sheet. Which method you choose depends on the material and whether or not there are seams. Gluing the full sheet usually makes for the best installation.

Preparation

Sheet flooring needs to "relax" before being installed, so unroll it and leave it face up in a room heated to around 70° F for at least 24 hours before installation. Then prepare the underlayment. It should be clean, dry, smooth, and free of any protruding nail heads. Remove the baseboards all around the room.

Layout

The best method for laying out and cutting resilient sheet flooring is to make a paper pattern of the kitchen floor and use it for a guide. Thin and flexible materials can be cut in place, but the pattern method gives the best results.

Make the pattern from any heavy paper that resists tearing, such as flooring felt or 15-pound building paper. Lay it out flat on the floor, overlapping the seams 3 or 4 inches. Tape the pieces together and trim the edges back about 1/2 inch from the walls—the edges do not have to be perfectly straight or parallel to the walls. Then cut small triangular openings (about 3 inches on a side) into the pattern every 3 or 4 feet and stick tape over them in such a way that it adheres to both the paper and the floor. This keeps the pattern from slipping as you move around on it.

Next mark an outline onto the pattern, just inside the edges, that exactly parallels all the walls, corners, cabinets, and other features that the flooring will abut. There are two ways to keep the outline exactly the same distance from the walls at all points. One is to place a yardstick or metal straightedge against the wall and trace a line against it onto the paper. Slide the straightedge along the wall as you go around the room marking the pattern. The second method is to use dividers or a scribing compass. Glide one leg of the compass along the wall and the other leg will leave a mark on the pattern. Use a setting that is easy to remember—2 inches, for instance—and tighten the set screw securely. Keep the compass perpendicular to the wall at all times. When the pattern is marked, remove all the pieces of tape that are holding it to the floor and carefully roll it up.

Cutting

Cut the sheet flooring, after it has relaxed, in a large area with a firm floor, such as a basement, garage, or driveway. The surface must be flat and clean. Lay the flooring face up, place the paper pattern over it, and align the pattern with the design printed on the flooring. Secure the pattern to the flooring by sticking tape over the triangular holes, just as you did when you secured it to the kitchen floor. If you used a scribing compass, retrace the outline you made on the pattern so that the compass leaves a scratch mark on the flooring that corresponds to the edges of the room. If you used a straightedge, lay it against the outline and trace a line onto the flooring with a ballpoint pen.

If the material will be loose-laid, check with the dealer to see whether a gap (usually 1/8 inch) should be left around the edges to allow for expansion, and cut accordingly.

Cut the material with a utility knife. Work slowly, using a straightedge to guide the blade. Place a scrap of plywood under the flooring to use as a cutting board.

For seams, leave 8 to 10 inches of extra material on the first piece. Lap the common edge of the second piece over it before cutting so that you can match up the design. Then place the paper pattern over the second piece so that it aligns with the first piece and cut around the perimenter.

Installation

Unroll the flooring in the kitchen and check the fit around the edges. Trim off any excess. If the flooring is loose-laid, simply staple the edges. Leave a 1/8-inch gap when you replace the baseboards. For full adhesion, carefully fold one half of the flooring back over itself, apply adhesive to the exposed underlayment, and lay the flooring back down over it. Use a flooring roller to smooth out the air bubbles. Then repeat the same process for the other side. Finally, go over the entire floor with the roller. Do not apply adhesive within 3 or 4 inches of a seam. Instead, when you set the second piece of flooring in place, match up the design pattern with the design on the first piece and then cut through both pieces at once along a straight line in the pattern. Glue down the second piece in the same way as you did the first. Spread adhesive under the seam and get it aligned before you do the rest of the piece. Wipe away any excess adhesive. Fuse the seam after the glue has set, using a seam sealer.

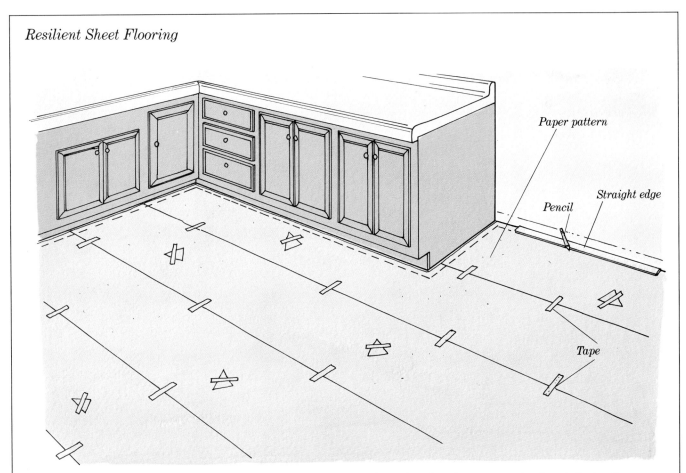

Paper pattern

Straight edge

Pencil

Tape

Installing Resilient Tile

Vinyl, rubber, cork, and other kinds of resilient tile are quite easy to install and offer you a chance to be creative with patterns.

Preparation

Like sheet flooring, resilient tile requires a smooth backing with tight, waterproof seams. Plan your entire layout prior to installation, but do not cut any tiles until all the full tiles are installed. That way you can cut each tile to an exact fit.

Layout

For a preliminary layout, snap two chalk lines centered between their respective walls. The first line should be parallel to the most prominent wall or feature in the room, and the second line should be perpendicular to the first. Lay out a row of tiles along each line. Fit them snugly and make adjustments so that the cut pieces will not be conspicuous. Then remove the tiles and renew the chalk lines.

Installation

Generally, you should install tiles from the center of the room, working out toward the walls. Position four tiles around the axis where the two chalk lines intersect. Then remove them, spread an adhesive recommended by the manufacturer in their place, and reset them in the adhesive. Align them carefully and wipe away any excess glue. Starting with the quadrant farthest from the door, continue to spread adhesive and lay tiles. Do a small section at a time until you learn how long it takes the adhesive to set up. If adhesive oozes up through a seam, wipe it off immediately with a clean rag, moistening the rag with water if necessary. There are special solvents that will remove the adhesive if it dries on the surface of the tile, but be careful not to let these solvents seep into the seams or they will destroy the bond. Use only full tiles and move out from the center toward the walls. Complete the other three quadrants in the same way as you did the first.

When you have set all of the full tiles, mark, cut, and install the border tiles. To mark a tile, place it upside down against the wall and scribe a line where it overlaps the full tile. This will make the border tiles fit flush against the wall. Measure and cut each border tile separately. Then apply the adhesive and set the tiles as described above. Finally, apply silicone sealant around the bases of all of the cabinets and built-in appliances. The adhesive should be dry within 24 hours; you can then install the baseboards and other moldings.

Installing Wood Floors

Most wood floors are installed, sanded, and given a coat or two of finish before the cabinets go in. Then, at the end of the project, the floor can be touched up and buffed, and the final coat of finish can be applied.

Some wood flooring requires specialized nailing machines and sanding equipment. Examples are 5/16-inch square-edge strip flooring or 3/4-inch unfinished tongue and groove. Although a competent do-it-yourselfer is certainly capable of renting the tools and installing this kind of floor, the work is tedious and defects are highly visible. You may want to hire professionals.

Prefinished hardwood flooring is easier to install. There are many types, some of which require nailing, notably 3/4-inch tongue and groove, for which you can rent a nailing machine to blind-nail the tongues. The simplest installation is 3/8-inch tongue-and-groove flooring applied with adhesive. Even though both types of flooring are prefinished, you should apply a final coat or two of finish to seal the joints and make the floor more durable for high-traffic kitchen use. Unless you can protect the surface during the rest of construction, it is best to install this type of floor at the end of the project.

Preparation

Wood flooring has a low moisture content and is subject to expansion and shrinkage. Avoid having the flooring delivered in the rain or snow, and make sure that all the plaster work and painting in the house has been finished. Store the wood near the kitchen in a dry room that is heated to at least 65° F. Stack the material log-cabin style or scatter it around the room. Then let it get acclimated for three to five days.

Wood flooring can be laid directly over the subfloor unless there is a crawl space or other unheated area directly underneath. In that case lay down 15-pound flooring felt to seal out moisture from below. Mark on the

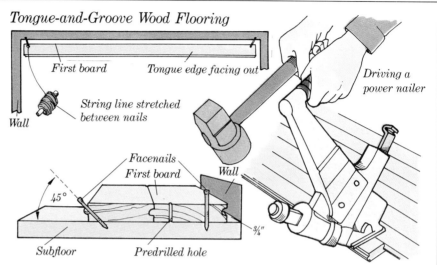

Tongue-and-Groove Wood Flooring

First board · Tongue edge facing out · Wall · String line stretched between nails · Driving a power nailer · 45° · Facenails · First board · Wall · Subfloor · Predrilled hole · 3/4"

wall the locations of the joists before you cover the subfloor with paper. Later you can snap chalk lines on the paper that will enable you to nail along the joists. If you are using adhesive, do not lay down paper. Instead, check the manufacturer's recommendations to see whether you should seal or prime the subfloor.

Layout

Always start strip and plank flooring at a wall. To establish a guideline along the starting wall, measure out 3/8 to 1/2 inch from the wall at each end, mark the floor, and snap a chalk line between the two marks. The gap provides for the expansion of the flooring; it will be covered by the baseboards. If the wall is not square with the rest of the room, you will have to adjust the starter line so that the flooring layout will be square. To determine whether the wall is square, measure the diagonals of the room.

Parquet flooring is installed in the same manner as resilient tile.

Installation

Sweep and vacuum the subfloor thoroughly. Lay out several rows of boards loosely on the floor and adjust them to achieve a random pattern of joints and the most attractive grain pattern. Begin each row with the cutoff piece from the previous row and leave a 3/8-inch to 1/2-inch gap at each end.

If you are nailing, align the first board with the groove along the chalk line, maintaining the gap at the end wall, and carefully facenail the board with 8d finishing nails at every joist and halfway between each joist. To prevent splits, predrill for each nail. Leave a 1/2-inch gap at the end of the row. Blind-nail the next two rows by hand, driving the nails into the tongue at a 45-degree angle. Nail at each joist. Stagger the end joints in a random pattern. Then use a nailing machine for the rest of the floor, standing so that your toes can hold down the board that is being nailed. When you reach the opposite wall, you may not have enough room to use the machine. Complete the nailing by hand.

If you are gluing, remove the first few rows of boards and spread the recommended adhesive on the subfloor, using a notched trowel. Work with the windows open, extinguish cigarettes and open flames, and follow any other safety precautions listed on the container. Spread only as much adhesive as you can cover with flooring before it sets up. Lay the first row in place, tongue out, and put shims between the wall and the boards to maintain the gap. As you lay the second row, tap the boards against the first row so that the tongues slide snugly into the grooves. You may have to rip-cut the last board to make it fit.

Installing Ceramic and Dimensioned Stone Tile

The tiles that are used on most home kitchen floors are thin, small, and even enough that they can be installed using a method known as thinsetting. Thinsetting is easy for a handy do-it-yourselfer.

Preparation

The subfloor and the backing for ceramic and dimensioned-stone tile must be sound, smooth, clean, and rigid. Do not apply tile over a surface that has give, because this will break the bond between the tile and the adhesive. The best backing for tile in a home kitchen is GMMU over a plywood subfloor.

To lay out tile you will need a chalk line, a straightedge, and a jury stick. A jury stick is a device that measures the widths of the tiles and the grout joints. You can make one out of a thin, straight board. Measure the width of your tiles and the width of your grout joints and mark these dimensions along the length of the board.

You'll need a 5-gallon bucket and special tile-mixing paddles to mix both the adhesive and the grout. You will also need a notched trowel to spread and comb the adhesive.

A beater board is an essential installation tool that you must make yourself. Cut a 2- or 3-foot length of 2 by 4 and cover one side of it with heavy felt or carpeting.

Three common cutting tools are used for tiles. To make small cuts, purchase a nipper. This tool resembles a pair of pliers, except that the jaws are strong enough to cut tiles. To make neat, straight cuts, use a snap cutter. If you have a lot of cuts, rent a wet saw equipped to cut tile.

For grouting you will need a rubber float, a margin trowel, and several good sponges. Be sure to have rags for cleanup and drop cloths to protect areas where adhesive and grout might splash. Wear a painter's mask when you work with adhesive and goggles when you cut tiles.

Layout

There are two overriding rules in arranging tiles. First, use as many full tiles and as few cut tiles as possible. Second, arrange the cut tiles to best advantage. Design your layout so that the focal points are set with full tiles.

Now, using a chalk line, snap a reference line across the floor, making sure that it is exactly parallel to the most prominent wall. Then snap another chalk line perpendicular to the first, so that the lines cross at precisely 90 degrees.

Starting from the axis where the reference lines intersect, use the jury stick to measure out the the number of tiles and joints you will need in each direction. When you get to the end of the line, there may not be enough space left to fit in a full tile. You have four options: Leave the row as it is and plan to cut a tile to fit; shift the row back and put the cut tile at the doorway; shift the row to allow cut tiles of equal size at both ends; slightly increase or decrease the width of all the grout joints. Choose whichever option you prefer and adjust the row accordingly. Snap a chalk line on the floor to mark the back edge of the last full tile in one direction. This line must be exactly perpendicular to the center chalk line, and it must be perfectly straight even if the wall is not square. Once you have planned the first row in each direction, you can align all the other rows with the first one.

It is very common for rooms to be slightly out of square. This will cause the space between the last row of full tiles and the nearby wall to be wider at one end than at the other. Make up the difference with tiles cut to fit exactly into the given space.

If, while determining your layout, you have made a major adjustment in the width of the grout joints, you may need to adjust the jury stick to allow for this adjustment. The width of the grout joints should be consistent throughout the installation.

Installing Full Tiles

Mix thinset adhesive according to the manufacturer's directions. Mix only the amount you will need to do one hour of setting at a time. Measure the liquid ingredients into a mixing bucket; then slowly add measured amounts of dry ingredients. Stir by hand or with special tile-mixing paddles. Avoid introducing air into the mixture, which will weaken the bond. Let the adhesive rest about 10 minutes before applying.

Thinset is applied in two steps. It is spread and it is combed. Use a notched trowel for both procedures.

Apply adhesive to a very small area, especially at first. Work along the reference lines. Stir the rested adhesive once or twice. Scoop a small amount onto the flat surface of the notched trowel. Holding the smooth edge of the trowel about 30 degrees off parallel, spread the adhesive on the surface to be tiled in a rounded, sweeping motion. Press the adhesive firmly into the backing materials, making sure that all areas are equally well covered and that no air bubbles have formed in the adhesive. Be sure to apply adhesive only in areas to be tiled, and do not cover any reference lines.

Combing is done with the notched edge of the trowel. Tilt this edge up about 45 degrees and comb the spread adhesive in two passes, in a crosshatch pattern.

The quality of the bond depends on the correct coverage of adhesive. The correct coverage depends on the depth of the ridges that are formed in the adhesive during combing. The depth of the ridges depends on the size of the notches and the angle at which the trowel is held.

To test the coverage, place one tile in the spread and combed adhesive. Push down gently with a slight twisting motion; then carefully lift the tile back up. Look at the back of the tile. It should be completely covered with adhesive. If any bisque shows through, the ridges are too shallow and you need to hold the trowel at less of an angle. If the adhesive has pushed well over the sides of the tile, the ridges are too deep and you should hold the trowel a little flatter.

Once you are confident that you are spreading and combing the adhesive correctly, begin setting the tiles in place. Place the first row right along your working line and use this row as a guide when you set successive rows.

Set the tiles into the adhesive firmly, with a slight twisting motion. You do not have to position them exactly at first. Once you have covered the spread adhesive with tiles, work to align them properly. Use the jury stick and special tile spacers to set the widths of the grout joints. Use a straightedge to align the tiles so that the grout joints will be straight across the field.

Once the tiles are properly aligned, hold the beater board on them and tap it lightly several times with a hammer to push the tiles firmly into the adhesive. Avoid hitting the beater board when it is raised above the tiles; this may send the board crashing into the tiles with enough force to break them. Use a carpenter's level to make certain that all of the tiles are flush.

Plastic tile spacers can be used to hold open the grout joints while you adjust the alignment and while the adhesive cures. They are available in a variety of sizes at tile retailers. Set the spacers between the tiles and at each point where four tiles come together.

Continue spreading and combing adhesive and placing and aligning tiles until all of the full tiles are set.

Cutting

To mark a tile for cutting, place one tile squarely on top of the last tile in the row and another tile on top of that one. Slide the top tile over the empty space, allowing for two grout lines. Using the top tile as a straightedge, draw a line across the middle tile. Cut along this line. Mark each tile and code it for reference. Cut all of the tiles at the same time.

Ceramic Tile Flooring

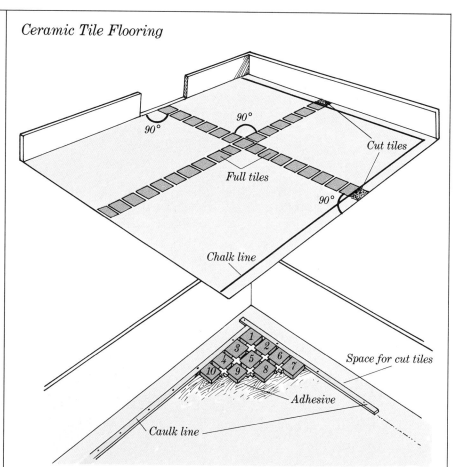

Installing Cut Tiles

Cut tiles and trim tiles are installed by a method called back-buttering. Use the trowel to spread adhesive across the back of each cut tile and set it in place, leaving space for the grout joints. Use the beater board to set the tile firmly in place. Check the alignment with the straightedge. Allow the adhesive to set the required length of time—usually 24 hours—before grouting. Avoid walking across the floor while the tiles set.

Grouting

Grout comes packaged in powder form. Mix it in a bucket, using special paddles, according to the manufacturer's directions. Avoid introducing air into the mixture. Let it rest for about 10 minutes. Remove tile spacers before you begin grouting.

Apply the grout with a rubber float or squeegee, dragging it diagonally across the tiles. Smooth the grout into the grout joints with a margin trowel, the end of a toothbrush handle, or a similar tool. Return the surplus grout to the bucket. All of the joints should be completely filled. Finish the joints to match across the entire run of tile.

Once the joints are filled, remove the excess grout from the face of the tiles with a clean, slightly damp sponge. Wipe the sponge in one direction, rinsing after each pass, until the surface is clean. When a hazy film appears on the surface of the tile, usually after about half an hour, polish it with cheesecloth. Avoid walking on the tiles for at least 24 hours after grouting, to allow for proper set up.

After about four weeks, apply a grout sealer to protect against staining and mildew.

INSTALLING APPLIANCES

Every type of major kitchen appliance is installed in a different way. The following techniques are intended to give you a general idea of how various appliances are installed. For your own installations, be sure to follow the manufacturer's instructions—not the promotional brochures.

Obtain these instructions when you order the appliances; don't wait until after delivery. You will need the information to rough in plumbing and wiring, to set cabinets, and to plan cutouts, all of which are usually done long before appliances are delivered.

If you have a septic system, and if you plan to install a dishwasher or a garbage disposer, make sure that the absorption field is adequate to accommodate these appliances, both of which use a lot of water. The Federal Housing Administration (FHA) and the Public Health Service recommend that the absorption field be 40 percent larger than minimum to accommodate a dishwasher, and 25 percent larger for a garbage disposer. The septic tank should also be larger than the normal minimum capacity—750 gallons instead of 500 gallons, for instance. Consult with local building or public health officials for specific requirements.

Installing Garbage Disposers

Turn off the water and the circuit breaker. Install the sink drain or—if there will be a disposer—the sink flange provided with it first. This flange includes a mounting bracket for the disposer and can be separated from the motor unit. You can install it before or after the sink is installed. Apply a bead of plumber's putty around the bottom of the rim to seal it against the sink. There is usually a large rubber or fiber gasket (or one of each) to go beneath the sink hole. The flange is held in place with a large slip nut, which you can tighten with channel-type pliers, or with three screws, which are tightened against the mounting bracket.

Prepare the garbage disposer. Attach the electrical cord by removing the cover plate and making the connections with wire nuts. Connect the drain elbow to the outlet. If you are connecting a dishwasher drain hose, remove the special knockout plug from inside the inlet.

Install the disposer. You may need someone to help you lift it into place and to hold it while you connect it to the mounting bracket. Most models have a quick-lock mechanism, which allows the disposer to hang loosely so that you can make adjustments while you hook up the plumbing. The drain hookup is a standard P-trap, and the dishwasher hose is connected to it with a hose clamp. Lock the disposer in place by tightening the set screws or cinching up a large ring. Then remove any debris from inside the unit, turn on the water and circuit breaker, plug the unit in, and test it.

There is no need to choose between gas and electric cooktops. Install both burner styles in one cooking area. A down-draft grill top completes the installation.

Installing Dishwashers

The rough-in connections for a dishwasher are usually made under the sink. They consist of a designated 110-volt electrical outlet with its own circuit breaker, a separate hot-water shutoff valve, and the 1½-inch sink drain. The dishwasher does not have to be next to the sink; the electrical cord and flexible supply and drain tubing can be run under or through adjacent cabinets. Most units are provided with a 6-foot drain hose, but this hose can be lengthened as specified by the manufacturer.

Most local codes require an air gap, usually mounted above the sink or countertop, to prevent the back flow of contaminated water and sewer gases into the dishwasher and possibly into the water supply system. Many newer dishwashers have an air gap built into them, but you may have to install an external one anyway. Some codes allow installation without an air gap if the drain hose is looped up and attached to the underside of the countertop.

Slide the dishwasher into place to test clearances. If new flooring is not yet installed, nail to the subfloor two long shims that equal the thickness of the finish floor. Locate them so that the dishwasher feet can slide on and off them without catching.

Remove the front access panel of the dishwasher. Locate the water supply inlet connection and mark its approximate location on the floor. Look all the way into the back of the dishwasher and note the best height for drilling holes through the cabinet wall to take the drain hose and the water supply tubing. The instructions will also provide a guide. Remove the dishwasher and drill holes at this location, as well as through the sides of any other cabinets between the sink and the dishwasher. Use a 1¼-inch bit for the drain hose; a ¾-inch bit for the supply tubing; and a 1-inch bit for the cord; or cut one hole large enough to take all three.

Install the hot-water supply tubing. Check the instructions to determine the required size of soft copper tubing. Usually it is ⅜-inch outside diameter, but sometimes it is ½-inch. Check also to see what fitting is needed to connect the tubing to the dishwasher. It is usually a ⅜-inch brass elbow, with male pipe threads at one end and a compression fitting at the other (MIP X Compression). Make sure that the outlet on the shutoff valve under the sink is for a compression fitting the same size as the tubing. Run the tubing from the shutoff valve along the back of the cabinets and a few inches above the floor in the dishwasher compartment, past the mark you made on the floor. Bend the tubing carefully to avoid kinks, using a tubing bender for tight turns. Connect it to the shutoff valve.

Prepare the dishwasher for installation. Change the front panel to the appropriate color. Attach a grounded electrical cord, with a plug, to the dishwasher, according to the instructions. Thread the end of the cord and the drain hose through the access hole and take up the slack as you slide the dishwasher into place.

Make the connections. Cut the supply tubing to length and connect it to the dishwasher. Connect the drain hose, which is typically ⅝-inch inside diameter but which may be ⁹⁄₁₆-inch inside diameter, to the inlet side of the air gap under the sink counter. Run a short section of ⅞-inch inside diameter drain hose from the outlet side of the air gap to the garbage disposer. If there is no disposer, you can buy a special drain tailpiece with a dishwasher waste fitting. Make sure that there are no kinks in the drain hose. Clamp it to the cabinets or countertop to prevent thumping. Lengthen the drain hose with a new piece by sliding both ends over a piece of copper tubing and securing them with clamps.

Plug in the dishwasher and run it through a test cycle. Screw the frame to the floor, if recommended, and attach the top of the unit to the underside of the countertop with the clip and screws provided with the unit.

Installing Cooktops

Cooktops designed for residential use are installed in much the same way as a sink; they require an opening in the countertop. Use the dimensions or the paper template specified by the manufacturer. Commercial gas cooktops sit on their own legs on a recessed countertop, which is often tiled. Steel guard strips or something similar are commonly used to protect the exposed cabinet sides. It is important to maintain all the specified clearances between the cooktop and the adjacent surfaces.

Turn off the gas and the circuit breaker. Prepare the gas or electrical rough-in connections. They should be in the cabinet below the cooktop, as close to the centerline as possible and no higher than the specified minimum distance below the cooktop. Local codes may specify how close the gas shutoff valve must be to the cooktop (typically 3 feet). You will need a flexible gas connector of the diameter specified by the manufacturer and of material approved by the local codes. Gas units also require a 120-volt electrical outlet for the electronic ignition device.

Electrical units require a separate 240-volt circuit, usually 30 or 40 amps, terminating in a box below the cooktop. Use flexible steel conduit or a heavy-duty appliance cord supplied with the cooktop to make the connection.

Mount the cooktop in the countertop opening. Apply plumber's putty or caulk around the edge of the opening first. Attach the unit from below with the clips, brackets, or screws provided.

Some electric models have a separate control panel that can be installed elsewhere on the countertop, in the front of the base cabinet, or on the wall cabinet at eye level. It comes with its own cable or wiring harness, which you can conceal behind the wall or in the cabinets. You may need an additional length, available from the supplier, for a long run.

ADDING FINISHING TOUCHES

T*he cabinets are in, the surfaces are covered, and all of the appliances are connected. The kitchen seems finished, and yet you have a sense that something is missing. Probably what is missing is the character and the individuality that make the kitchen yours.*

It's time now to install the finishing touches—the elements that tie everything together and reflect your own personal style. Some of these elements are functional accessories—things that are common to every kitchen but that offer opportunities for your creative touch. Others are features that are designed to meet your special needs. Others are purely decorative elements that make a house a home.

Don't choose these accessories as an afterthought. Both functional and purely decorative accessories need careful planning. How much space will they require? What colors, sizes, textures, and styles do you prefer? Price is also a major factor—especially at the end of a long and expensive project. Remember to budget in these accessories at the beginning. Then again, you may prefer to add them later, once you have got the feel of your new room.

Little projects are sometimes the most impressive. Piano hinges hold this occasional table and allow the bracing legs to fold back against the wall. Down, it is completely out of the way. Up, it's a handy extra countertop.

Installing Overhead Racks

There are many ways to display pots, pans, and cooking utensils and keep them handy for quick use. Racks can be mounted on the wall or ceiling. You can choose a prefabricated rack or you can have a rack custom-made by a local welding shop. Or, build your own rack, using decorative hooks attached to a strip of hardwood stained to match the cabinets.

Installing a rack is easy. Depending on the design, it will be supported on mounting brackets, hooks for chains, or flanges for suspension rods. Simply attach these to the ceiling or the wall. Be sure to attach them to framing members. Toggle bolts driven through the wallboard will not support a heavy rack of pans.

Installing Towel Bars

Plan to install bars for both cloth and paper towels wherever they will be most convenient. You may want to conceal them behind doors or under cabinets to avoid a cluttered look, or you might prefer the splashes of color provided by a display of decorative

towels. Choose towel bars to add a touch of opulence, an accent of bright color, or an emphasis on clean, crisp lines. To install them, drill holes into the wall studs, into the wallboard, or into the cabinets and attach the towel rods with screws. If you are attaching them to the wallboard, use expansion shields.

Installing Window Treatments

Mini-blinds offer a popular and practical way to dress up windows and provide privacy. The sleek surfaces are fairly easy to wipe clean and the horizontal lines harmonize with a contemporary decor. Shutters are also practical and impart a more traditional look, although they are more difficult to clean. Curtains can be used to soften the hard edges of cabinets and appliances, but it is hard to keep curtains spotless in a kitchen. Many homeowners prefer to leave the kitchen windows bare if privacy is not an issue. They brighten the room and make the most of any view. Whatever your choice, install the window coverings in the same way as you would in any other room.

Installing Hidden Accessories

Ironing boards, televisions, and pet-feeding centers are only some of the surprises that can lurk behind innocent kitchen facades. Some hidden accessories can be installed in cabinets—tables or ironing boards, for instance, that fold up into a standard cabinet drawer. Others come in self-contained units that can be recessed into the wall.

Storage systems are available from cabinet manufacturers and specialized retailers. And, of course, there is a creative custom solution to meet almost any storage need.

To install prefabricated components, attach the mounting brackets inside the cabinets or to the framing, following the manufacturer's instructions. You may have to alter a cabinet or an alcove slightly.

Having a Party

When you finally move into the new kitchen, mark the event with a celebration. It can be an elaborate party or a simple, special family meal. The important thing is to bring an end to the process. Once you have done that, the project feels finished, even if there are still a few nagging details left to tidy up. Then you are free to enjoy the final product—and to reward yourself for all those months of planning and effort.

Plan and execute the storage systems inside cabinets and drawers while designing and constructing your new kitchen. Custom spice racks and other specialty items that meet your cooking needs will increase your satisfaction with the finished room.

PHOTOGRAPHY ACKNOWLEDGMENTS

Homeowners

Special thanks to the following people for their generous hospitality in allowing us to photograph their kitchens.

Lois Arnold
Agnes Bourne and
 James Luebbers, MD
James and Pamela Cameron
Kati and John Casida
Michael and Diane Cenko
Eleanor R. Crary
Claude and Mary Daughtry
Kathy and Phil Doherty
Glen and Judy Harrington
Brooke and Kurt Hauch
Jim and Leslie Haydel
Hilda and Seymour Kessler
Janet Kirschen
Loni Kuhn
Sandra Lam
Nancy and Tom Mavrides
Barbara and Howard Norton
Cynthia Peddie
Mr. and Mrs. Alfred V. Sanguinetti
Susan Schapiro
Carolyn and Jim Sconza
Gary and Cherie Semans
Sally Spencer and Phil Pollock
Siri Lee Swan

Industrial shelving in this walk-in pantry provides plenty of storage for home-made canned goods and bulk food.

Featured Kitchens

Special thanks to the following individuals and businesses for allowing us to photograph their work.

Front cover, page 62
Designer and Builder: Homeowners with Bob Johnson

Pages 1,18, 22
Designer: Carlene Anderson
Builder: Dick Kowalski, West Build

Pages 3, 8
Designer: Homeowner with Lyndell Hogan, House of Kitchens
Builder: Phil Hendrix, Village Builders

Pages 5, 28, 84, back cover (top left)
Architect: Jerry Lee and Pam Lee, LDA Architects
Builder: Tony Ng
Cabinets: Jim Martin, Lignum Vitae

Pages 6, 104, back cover (bottom right)
Designer and Builder: Betty Sundborg, Marin Kitchen Works

Page 9
Designer: Robert Idol, ASID
Builder: Blair Alexander

Pages 11, 106
Designer: Pamela Cameron, Uniquely Yours; Paul Kline, House of Kitchens
Builder: Wilson Way Builders

Pages 12, 107
Designer: Lynn Augstein Design Services
Builder: House of Kitchens; Wilson Way Builders

Pages 14, 74
Architect: William Duval
Builder: Jonathan Allen

Pages 15, 34
Designer: Michael McCutcheon; Carolyn Sell, House of Kitchens
Builder: McCutcheon Construction

Page 21
Designer: Agnes Bourne, ASID
Builder: Thomas Saxton, Saarman Construction

Page 24
Designer and Builder: Superior Home Remodeling

Pages 26, 27, 81
Designer: Phyliss Silver Interiors; House of Kitchens
Builder: David Wilson, Wilson Way Builders

Pages 33, 97
Designer: Paul Kline, House of Kitchens
Builder: David Wilson, Wilson Way Builders

Pages 37, 58, 59, 60
Designer: Homeowner
Builder: Kelly Hale, Hale Remodeling

Pages 38, 40, 41, 42, 43, back cover (top right)
Architect: James Miller AIA and Associates
Cabinets: Jim Martin, Lignum Vitae

Pages 44, 45
Designer: Beverly Wilson
Builder: Odin's Hammer, Inc.

Pages 46, 47, 49, 64, back cover (bottom left)
Designer: House of Kitchens
Builder: Homeowner

Pages 50, 51, 52, 53
Designer: Carlene Anderson
Builder: T.W. Heyenga

Pages 56, 57
Designer: Carlene Anderson
Builder: John Wilkins, Custom Kitchens

Page 69
Designer: Agnes Bourne, ASID
Builder: Yuke Muramoto
Faux finish: Shelly Masters Studio

Pages 70, 71
Designer and Builder: John Wilkins, Custom Kitchens

Page 73
Designer: Homeowner with House of Kitchens
Builder: David Wilson, Wilson Way Builders
Neon Sculpture: Josie Crawford

Page 90
Designer: House of Kitchens; John Zanakas; Barbara Wolfe Interiors
Builder: Tom Herrick, Rehabitat

INDEX

W, X, Y, Z

U.S./Metric Measure Conversion Chart

	Formulas for Exact Measures				*Rounded Measures for Quick Reference*		
	Symbol	*When you know:*	*Multiply by:*	*To find:*			
Mass (Weight)	oz	ounces	28.35	grams	1 oz		= 30 g
	lb	pounds	0.45	kilograms	4 oz		= 115 g
	g	grams	0.035	ounces	8 oz		= 225 g
	kg	kilograms	2.2	pounds	16 oz	= 1 lb	= 450 g
					32 oz	= 2 lb	= 900 g
					36 oz	= 2¼ lb	= 1000 g (1 kg)
Volume	tsp	teaspoons	5.0	milliliters	¼ tsp	= 1/24 oz	= 1 ml
	tbsp	tablespoons	15.0	milliliters	½ tsp	= 1/12 oz	= 2 ml
	fl oz	fluid ounces	29.57	milliliters	1 tsp	= ⅙ oz	= 5 ml
	c	cups	0.24	liters	1 tbsp	= ½ oz	= 15 ml
	pt	pints	0.47	liters	1 c	= 8 oz	= 250 ml
	qt	quarts	0.95	liters	2 c (1 pt)	= 16 oz	= 500 ml
	gal	gallons	3.785	liters	4 c (1 qt)	= 32 oz	= 1 liter
	ml	milliliters	0.034	fluid ounces	4 qt (1 gal)	= 128 oz	= 3¾ liter
Length	in.	inches	2.54	centimeters	⅜ in.	= 1 cm	
	ft	feet	30.48	centimeters	1 in.	= 2.5 cm	
	yd	yards	0.9144	meters	2 in.	= 5 cm	
	mi	miles	1.609	kilometers	2½ in.	= 6.5 cm	
	km	kilometers	0.621	miles	12 in. (1 ft)	= 30 cm	
	m	meters	1.094	yards	1 yd	= 90 cm	
	cm	centimeters	0.39	inches	100 ft	= 30 m	
					1 mi	= 1.6 km	
Temperature	°F	Fahrenheit	5/9 (after subtracting 32)	Celsius	32° F	= 0° C	
					68°F	= 20°C	
	°C	Celsius	9/5 (then add 32)	Fahrenheit	212° F	= 100° C	
Area	in.^{2}	square inches	6.452	square centimeters	1 in.^{2}	= 6.5 cm^2	
	ft^2	square feet	929.0	square centimeters	1 ft^2	= 930 cm^2	
	yd^2	square yards	8361.0	square centimeters	1 yd^2	= 8360 cm^2	
	a.	acres	0.4047	hectares	1 a.	= 4050 m^2	